Healing Prayer
and
Medical Care

Healing Prayer
and
Medical Care

GOD'S HEALTHCARE PLAN

ABBY ABILDNESS

DESTINY IMAGE® PUBLISHERS, INC.
P.O. Box 310, Shippensburg, PA 17257-0310
"Speaking to the Purposes of God for This Generation and for the Generations to Come."

This book and all other Destiny Image, Revival Press, MercyPlace, Fresh Bread, Destiny Image Fiction, and Treasure House books are available at Christian bookstores and distributors worldwide.

For a U.S. bookstore nearest you, call 1-800-722-6774.
For more information on foreign distributors, call 717-532-3040.
Reach us on the Internet: www.destinyimage.com.

Trade Paper ISBN 13: 978-0-7684-3590-0
Hardcover ISBN 978-0-7684-3591-7
Large Print ISBN 978-0-7684-3592-4
Ebook ISBN 978-0-7684-9055-8

For Worldwide Distribution, Printed in the U.S.A.
1 2 3 4 5 6 7 8 9 10 11 / 13 12 11 10

Acknowledgments

Special thanks to our core healing team that has been faithful to establish the medical center prayer service and to minister their hearts and prayers to bring healing to the lives of many. May the Lord multiply your efforts and prayers. And thanks to the many who have joined us in this ministry.

Thank you Dr. Jim Abildness, Janet Roberts, Kim and Mike Sadowski, Jodi Enoch, Janice Slaybaugh, Jane and Itaya Bryan, Randy Maulfair, Bill and Lorrie Diggins, Dennis Kennel, Jarred Miller, Donna Beaver, Lori Kime, Beth and Mike Kelly, Carol Lehman, Terri Binnette, Lisa Sensenig, and Melanie Chandler.

Endorsements

The timely wisdom and insight regarding the healthcare industry, in *Healing Prayer and Medical Care,* is revolutionary. It has the potential to unlock transformation throughout the medical world. Receive and get equipped with God's strategy for healthcare, as Abby clearly reveals Jesus' heart for healing in every sphere of life. This book is a must read, for we are all effected by the medical industry.

Ché Ahn
Senior Pastor, HROCK Church, President and Founder,
Harvest International Ministry

Healing Prayer and Medical Care is an insider's view of the power of God working in and through "healing teams" in clinical and nonclinical settings. Abby tells us, "The wisdom of God planted where the wisdom of medicine flourishes brings the best security to know that human wisdom is boosted by God's wisdom and healing power" (Chapter 6). If I could summarize this engaging book in a succinct statement it would be, "The power of God, is available to the people of God, to achieve the purposes of God!" Congratulations, Abby, your testimonies of divine healing and the healing power of God's unconditional love, as well as your insights on the healing power of forgiveness will certainly equip your readers for the ministry of miracles.

Dr. Alan N. Keiran, captain, Chaplain Corps, USN (ret.)
Chief of Staff, Office of the U.S. Senate Chaplain
Author of *Take Charge of Your Destiny*, Destiny Image, 2008

In today's world, and in the Body of Christ, we need a wedding to occur between the various branches of the healing arts. We need the natural and the supernatural brought together like two praying hands. That is what Abby is doing for us in her new book! I applaud her efforts and want to see more holistic approaches to life come forth as exhibited in this down to earth, practical, and yet inspirational read!

James W. Goll
Encounters Network • Prayer Storm • Compassion Acts
Author of *The Seer, The Lost Art of Intercession,* and many more

"For many years, Abby Abildness has been raising up and deploying a growing army of healing warriors. In love they have touched many lives in our region and other parts of the world with the restoring presence of the Lord. In the following pages, you will be touched by the healing heart of our Great Physician. You will read stories that will inspire you to trust Him more. You will be stirred with fresh insight into His healing ways.

Thanks, Abby, for this timely book. Let the healing army arise!"

Dave Hess
Pastor, Christ Community Church, Harrisburg, Pennsylvania
Author of *Hope Beyond Reason*

Having been a friend and ministry associate with Abby Abildness, and her husband, Dr. Jim Abildness, it is with honor that

I am recommending to your library *Healing Prayer and Medical Care: God's Healthcare Plan.*

From the times that we have met with her with the state governor, senators, and many meetings together in the past that included delegations received from Iraq and congressional symposiums, the Lord made it very clear to me that Abby has the anointing of God for favor in many circles, but all include healing in the heart, soul, mind, and body. God has clearly equipped Abby with the clear guidelines we in the Christian faith must adhere—healing and healthcare are in concert!

From her vast background as an intercessor, prophetic seer, and connector, Abby will cause you to learn that from her steadfast faithfulness of praying for the sick, obeying the call to steward God's Word in healing, and, yes, hospital and medical healthcare practices, she is the person I believe has God's gift to literally demonstrate the "Healing Tree" in Revelation. Abby, by God's design, has offered us God's plan is faith, and that healthcare does not contradict, but complements our faith to accept our complete healing—body, mind, and soul! Abby will give you a clear, tested, and proven guide in *Healing Prayer and Medical Care: God's Healthcare Plan,* that will not leave you without answers when your miracle does not occur on your timetable with what others has told you must occur or you do not practice faith! She shows us that healing and healthcare with God's truthfulness does not leave you speechless, yet offers healing for every part of your life now and for eternity. I highly recommend to you *Healing Prayer and Medical Care: God's Healthcare Plan* as a guide for your library of faith, complete with transparency that our Church must employ for total healing.

Always a Voice for God,
John Mark Pool, author and co-founder of
Word to the World Ministries
www.w2wmin.org

What can God do if we pursue His heart for healing with humility and boldness? *Healing Prayer and Medical Care* will inspire your faith and imagination! Abby and her family consistently and creatively minister to the poorest as well as to international leaders and heads of state. The testimonies of miraculous healings and whole life restorations are simply breathtaking. Clear, practical insights can release your desire to reach out in your own way as part of Heaven's great redemption toward the suffering and lost. As their pastor and friend for over ten years, I heartily recommend the authenticity of the lives and the true stories you are about to encounter.

Charles Stock, Senior Pastor
Life Center Ministries International
Harrisburg, Pennsylvania

My wife, Abby, is uniquely suited to write a book on healing prayer and medical care. She has a history in the medical field as a licensed occupational therapist with a master's degree and worked in a clinical setting in a rehabilitation hospital and in the Hershey Medical Center. She also worked with a joint college professor appointment with Elizabethtown College and Penn State Hershey Medical Center. And she did postgraduate training in marriage and family therapy and taught in Myerstown Theological Seminary. She is an ordained pastor and founded and directs an international Healing Network of leaders impacting medical, business, pastoral, and government leaders.

She has experienced miraculous healing in her own body after being diagnosed with infertility and being prayed over for healing, and since having four healthy children of her own. She witnessed many miraculous healings through the prayers of others, and has seen her own prayers answered for physical healing as well as emotional and relational healing for people in this country and other nations. Her faith in Jesus as Jehovah Rapha, the God who heals, has not disappointed her, but rather strengthened her faith in Him to do the impossible. He is a great God. The Bible says, "Only believe and you will see him to great things." In this book, Abby describes how she and others step out in faith and witness God bring healing because He is a loving God who has the power to heal since He is the same yesterday, today, and forever.

Dr. James Abildness

Contents

Preface

Having been in healthcare and "God-care" for the past 30 years, I value healthcare and God-care and want to see a responsible balance so that the way of treating the body, mind, and spirit would bring healing to the whole person and their family life. We see many people in the hospital that have their lives in a healthcare crisis crying out to God for His healing touch for their hearts, relationships, and bodies. Often their despair goes beyond the healthcare diagnosis to a fundamental cry to God for help in their time of need. It is a prime opportunity to minister and impact a life forever touched by God's loving care for their emotional and spiritual concerns at a time of critical need.

Introduction

Now may the God of peace Himself sanctify you completely; and
may your whole spirit, soul, and body be preserved blameless at
the coming of our Lord Jesus Christ (1 Thessalonians 5:23).

The healing fruit of the God of Peace purifies us and separates us from ill health, aligning us to wholeness of spirit, soul, and body. This causes us to live in health and well-being. In Exodus 23:25 God said, *"You shall serve the Lord your God, and He will bless your bread and water. And I will take sickness away from the midst of you."* After 30 years' experience as a behavioral health specialist praying for healing, I have observed that greater healing comes as people have made peace with God and His purposes in their lives. God uses the suffering seasons of our lives to draw us closer to Him as we cry out for His help. And He brings those sufferings to nothing in comparison with the glory that is revealed in our living testimonies.

I notice in my world travels that you can see patterns in sickness in regions according to the spiritual and environmental problems in the region. Prayers targeted at those regional issues will heal roots of sickness for nations and families within the nations. And they will bring prosperous results in health and well-being. Combining healing prayer and medical care can bring God's healing care to society around the world.

I will share stories and strategies of healing prayer that draw people to healing and the heart of God. Jesus brought the good news of the Gospel in story form to demonstrate the working of His coming kingdom. So I will use his teaching model as I deal with some of the issues in balancing believing prayer and medical diagnosis and treatment:

1. Ministering to unbelievers in crisis
2. Finding a balanced prescription for healing
3. Finding healing in worship
4. Healing from the heart of God
5. Healing in communion with God and one another
6. Healing in the Word (see Exod. 15:26)
7. Healing faith (see Heb. 11)

After five years leading a healing prayer service in the chapel of Penn State University's Milton S. Hershey Medical Center and praying with medical staff and families on a weekly basis, I have seen a pervasive sense that God is bringing powerful answers to prayer for patients, families, and medical staff. Word has spread that "God stories" are being shared around nursing desks throughout the hospital, and people are discussing God stories in the halls of the medical center. There is an increasing awareness in the medical community that healing prayer provides faith benefits that boost medical healing results. For example, a Jewish surgeon went to operate on a tumor, but in surgery he discovered it had disappeared. After prayer, he double-checked on the scans even in the surgical room. He admitted that though he wasn't one to utilize healing prayer, his praying nurse had gotten one of "those miracles" for which she prayed.

Another surgeon went to put a tracheotomy into a premature baby and noticed the baby was breathing on her own and didn't need the tracheotomy tube after prayer. An orthopedic surgeon who had cancer himself had been "lit up" with cancer cells on his CAT scans. He had a grim diagnosis that medicine had no further alternatives to help. But he found, one week after prayer ministry, that his body was clear of any cancer cells. He exclaimed he had gotten a miracle and that the humanities department he had helped to establish hadn't gotten this kind of healing result to body, mind, and spirit without healing prayer. For other examples, there are patients with neurological injuries that doctors said would never recover due to spinal damage or head trauma. We have seen some of these comatose patients healed to the point of walking out of the hospital.

This is a hospital with distinguished doctors who have excellent diagnostic skills. But some patients are healing beyond what medicine is capable of due to healing prayers boosting healing results. Our healing team honors the university setting and supports doctors and their treatments with prayer. Now that word has spread to the surrounding community, some patients tell us they choose this hospital and intentionally schedule doctor visits on Fridays in order to combine healing prayer with their medical treatment schedule. Some cancer patients say they want a healing prayer infusion before their chemotherapy infusions.

Some medical staff refer their patients for healing prayer, knowing that they can count on it to be there on a regular, weekly basis. We have discovered a great benefit to all involved from having lay pastoral care prayer ministers available in the chapel where concerned family and staff come for solace and cry out for help from God. This combination brings the greatest healing for body, soul, and spirit for all.

In the medical and religious communities, differing beliefs and views on the benefits of healing prayer and medicine have caused breaches in the strength and partnership that they could experience for the greatest benefit to patients. If prayer ministers honor the medical setting and its regulations and medical staff honor the prayer ministers coming to help the pastoral care, there can be strength to both believing prayer teams and medical teams for the best holistic care for all concerned. My heart is to see healing prayer offered as part of the routine treatment in medical care facilities everywhere for those patients, family, and staff who would like to partake of it and get the fullest healing benefit to their health. I would also promote prayer services in other secular settings to bring the wellspring of God right into the community to minister to the needs of people where they are. It is a model Jesus used as He went through the towns, teaching and ministering, taking healing love to those who came for a healing touch.

The biggest miracle is the love of God that transforms lives daily as they receive a healing touch to their hearts and souls. It convinces hurting people of God's loving concern for them. It is a taste of Heaven that makes them want more of God in their daily lives. It is a reviving wellspring of reviving revelation and healing.

Our healing prayer team thanks Pastor Paul Derricksen, co-ordinator of the pastoral care department and chaplaincy school, under whose auspices we offer the ecumenical Christian weekly meditative worship and healing prayer service in the chapel as pastoral care volunteers. We also thank Kathy Martin, pastoral care receptionist, who helped us logistically and enjoyed hearing the healing testimonies in people's lives.

We appreciate the deep healing work of the pastoral care department as they come alongside patients and families helping them work through the stages of sickness and suffering, and grief. And we appreciate the daily work of healthcare professionals tirelessly ministering healing to patients. We count it a privilege to come alongside the staff as we minister in the hospital chapel and when we are called to the bedside of patients.

Chapter 1

Prayer Service in a Medical Center

"Come to Me and I will give you Rest"

In the center of the Penn State Hershey Medical Center Chapel flows a fountain with three small stones on it. It flows quietly with a rippling effect as families in distress turn into the chapel to say a quick prayer for God's help before they go for their medical test or treatment or while they wait for their loved one in surgery or in Intensive Care. Some pray for a miracle, some pray for a second chance at life, some ask for God's mercy. They all cry out to God for help in their time of distress. Medical staff take a quick break in the chapel, too. They need wisdom and strength for their busy lives and caseloads. They all have one thing in common—a busy, stressed life, with their own lives or family members' lives in the balance, needing God's help. They come with a prayer in their hearts to ask for God's help. For anyone in times of need, the chapel is open as a welcoming place of refuge and strength. And God's redeeming love is there for them.

The Healing Tree International and Aglow International prayer teams have brought together prayer ministers from the regional pastor's network of churches in the surrounding cities. An announcement goes out over the hospital intercom, and there is a sign outside the chapel to invite passersby to come in to the Christian meditative worship and healing prayer service. All patients, families, and staff are welcome. The sign beckons them into the chapel: *Come to Me, all who are weary and heavy-laden, and I will give you rest* (Matthew 11:28 NASB).

As people are drawn to get God's help in the chapel by their serious medical, financial, and family needs, they are surprised and relieved to find a healing prayer team ready to care for them in an atmosphere of meditative worship. Distressed people come into the holy, soothing, worshipful presence of God and find rest and rejuvenation for their weary souls. Many people are moved to tears as they walk in and sense a special presence of God. They open their hearts to begin to share their stories of need to caring prayer ministers. Healing Team Prayer ministers ask how they can pray for the concerns on their hearts, which may be their sick loved ones, their medical caregivers, their finances, or their family members feeling estranged from God and questioning what He is doing. They ask for peace and strength, wisdom, and finances in their time of crisis. Many ask for miracles and healing and a second chance at life. Deep ministry to their hearts and souls happens in their time of need. It begins to open up heart wounds that bring healing. They often share beyond the physical healing needs because of the concerns that pour out of their hearts in their distinct time of need.

People are delighted to discover they are not alone as they ask for God's help. Some already have faith and are coming to pray to the God they know. Many have been away from God but in their desperation are asking for His help in time of need. They find gracious, caring prayer ministers to help them pray and listen to their fears and concerns. They gain a sense of God's loving care as they find God would have others available to come alongside them and pray.

Place to Share Concerns

In the calming atmosphere, people often share of their concerns that magnify the prayer needs in this time of health crisis. For many, it is a first time to get this kind of personal prayer support, and they are moved to tears as they pour out their concerns before God. This kind of help in a critical time brings an emotional and spiritual healing that they will never forget. Quite a good number come back to the chapel even after they are discharged to give thanks in the chapel to God and to the prayer team.

For some, the trauma of an injury brings a time of reconciling in their lives. For example, a young man speeding on his motorcycle—running from responsibilities in life, drinking and doing drugs, running from God and family problems—suddenly crashes, and his leg is crushed so badly it needs to be amputated. Now, as he's sitting in the hospital with his bandaged, amputated leg, his sister gathers prayer for healing of his body, mind, and spirit. She calls for prayer for him to stop running and for his life to be healed and restored. She had even been praying for his soul to be at peace with God. Now he sits in his hospital bed after the motorcycle accident, jolted into the reality of his messed-up life. He knows he has been running and wants to get his life in order but doesn't know how. He has come to a fork in the road over how he has been living his life and where to go from here with an amputated leg.

Inspired by his sister's love for him, the prayer team is called to pray in the medical center chapel around those rippling waters at the symbolic fountain of life. A small team prays and prepares to go with his sister to his room. One who joined the team that day is a new believer who rides a motorcycle and gains a heart to come alongside and be a friend who can mentor this young man as he hears his story. The team soon goes to his room, inspired by the love of God they gain for him in prayer. They find the young man in his room ready to make a decision before God to change his life and come to God, who he knows he has been avoiding. He is desperate to find help for his life and eager to pray for God's help. He is grateful to find a new friend who he can call upon to finally get his life on the right road.

Place to Make Decisions About Life

The fountain in the chapel becomes a place where people make decisions about which direction they will take their lives. *The tragedies put before the Lord Jesus in prayer become triumphs of life in getting on the right road.* Often, believing family members pray for their whole families to come to stronger faith in God and for His help in time of need. The prayers at the altar often bring families closer together as they need to strengthen one another to cope with the crisis.

Some families make decisions in the chapel about releasing a loved one. Some have to decide about taking a loved one off of life support. And some find a new faith to pray for healing beyond what medicine would know to do. They find that Jesus prayers bring a miraculous healing. They rejoice and know the God of the universe is working on their behalf. A wellspring of healing blessings from God happen at what becomes an altar of prayer in the medical center chapel to help the sick and needy heal and make it through a time of great need.

Place for Speaking Life-giving Words

The healing prayer team is ready with Jesus prayers and life-giving words. God speaks in his Word, *"…I have set before you life*

and death, blessing and cursing; therefore choose life, that both you and
your descendants may live" (Deut. 30:19). We do this by honoring
and obeying His commandments. In the place of distress we can
choose life and choose it abundantly. Praying for God's help, we
can find a wellspring of wisdom from God, ministering His love,
peace, and comfort. We receive life-giving words that sustain us
and guide us at a critical time—words that will be remembered
because they were spoken into us at a key point in life where there
was deep emotional and spiritual need. Deep speaks to deep. The
deep things of God speak to deep needs of the heart. God inspires
His people to minister His word and wisdom as a wellspring of
life, flowing from the loving heart of God to restore His beloved
people in need.

Place to Minister to Non-Christians

One day a Muslim man came to the medical center chapel altar
to observe our Christian prayers. He knew we met every Friday
right before the Muslim Friday prayers. He knew we had an altar
of prayer to Jesus, and his group used the same altar every Friday
to pray to Allah. He came early for his Friday Muslim prayers to
see what we were doing. As he sat and watched, a middle-aged
man came in, distressed about his mother who had had a massive
heart attack. The doctors didn't expect her to live. The troubled
man was visibly anxious and smelled of smoke, trying to calm
himself with cigarettes. Desperate for help, he came to the chapel
though he wasn't one normally to go for God's help.

The team greeted him and showed Jesus' compassion for his
grief over his mother's life. We prayed for a spirit of peace to
rest on him and for God to be with his mother. As we prayed he
calmed down and apparently had a surprising vision, because he
exclaimed with excitement, "I see a bright neon light flashing,
Jesus is Lord, Jesus is Lord, Jesus is Lord!" Then he said, "I need
to get Jesus. How do I get Him? I felt His deep love, and I need

it desperately. I want Jesus. I see He is my help as I cry for my mother. I want to receive Jesus in my heart." The team prayed with him, and his visage changed from distress to the joy of the Lord, even though he hadn't heard of any change in his mother's condition. His spirit was revived to have strength to face the condition of his mother. And he received prayer that his hands would bring a healing touch to his mother's heart.

Now the Muslim man watched and was amazed to see the dramatic change in the distressed man. The Muslim man was so impressed by witnessing Jesus ministering to the now joyful man that for the next few Fridays he kept coming early for his Muslim prayer time so he could experience more of our Jesus prayers. He and his Muslim friends knew that Jesus healed. They said there is more in the Qur'an about Jesus' life and healings than there is about Mohammed.

We offered him a Jesus prayer for healing of his chronic headache he'd had for years. When we prayed over him, the chronic headache immediately left him. Surprised by the healing, he asked what trick we had done to do that. We said there was no trick; Jesus truly healed him. Each week, he kept coming back. He saw more people being ministered to and more healings. After awhile, he said he would be returning to Pakistan and wanted our prayers for peace and safety on his flight, since he was afraid of flying. We prayed the Aaronic blessing over him: *"The Lord bless you and keep you; the Lord make His face shine upon you, and be gracious to you; the Lord lift up His countenance upon you, and give you peace"* (Num. 6:24-26). He gained a noticeable sense of peace over his fear of flying. He came back the next week to say how he observed how unusually strong God was with our ministry. And he wanted to bless us for blessing him. So he spoke a blessing over us when he returned.

Interestingly, we had been told by the hospital chaplain that we could lose favor for our ministry in the chapel if we evangelized people, because that would anger them in their time of need. But Jesus gave His own Gospel message Himself in a delightful way that drew increased faith in both the Muslim man and the distressed man.

> *Ho! Everyone who thirsts, come to the waters; and you who have no money, come, buy and eat...let your soul delight itself in abundance* (Isaiah 55:1-2).

Mark Siljander has studied the essence of the struggle of Christians evangelizing Muslims in his book, *A Deadly Misunderstanding: A Congressman's Quest to Bridge the Muslim-Christian Divide.* He believes Jesus came to uphold and fulfill the Jewish Scriptures, not to contradict or supersede them.[1] *"Do not think that I came to destroy the Law or the Prophets. I did not come to destroy but to fulfill"* (Matt. 5:17). Jesus saw His own teaching as a continuation of existing Scripture, just as Mohammed evidently saw the Qur'an and his own teaching as a continuation of the existing Scriptures. As Paul spoke in Athens, *"Therefore, the One whom you worship without knowing, Him I proclaim to you,"* the Lord Jesus does this in a refreshing way for many as He touches their need in the chapel (Acts 17:23).

Place of Safety, Refuge, and Healing

The Penn State Hershey Medical Center interfaith chapel was built to be a place of safety, refuge, and healing for all people of all faiths. It is carefully designed as an interfaith chapel with sections for the Muslims to pray, the Jews to pray, and the Christians to pray. It has beautiful glass art in the corridor entering the chapel, showing its ministry to people in all stages of life, from birth to death. The glass doorway to the chapel has a built-in wooden tree with healing leaves etched in green glass surrounding the glass door, representing the leaves of healing for all the nations. Rippling waters flow in its center fountain to exemplify the river of life flowing in the chapel—God's space in the center of the trauma hospital. The prayers at that altar within the hospital call on God to bring His presence from the throne of God through the river of life to bring the healing to the nations (see Rev. 22:2). It flows in the spirit of prayer into that whole facility to minister on every floor and in every room of the hospital. It flows to meet every need with every patient in their beds, calling out for God's help in the way that they understand to do. Psalms 103:3 reveals that He forgives all our iniquities and He *heals all* our diseases. None is too difficult for God to heal.

Place of Personal Refreshment

The chapel meditative worship brings a peaceful sense of cleansing and refreshment as people sit on chairs surrounding the fountain to pray to God. The spiritual well revives life when it is found in the dry and thirsty seasons of life. Just as Jesus met the Samaritan woman at the well and told her He had life-giving water that would bring life forevermore to her troubled life (having been through five husbands), so does this chapel healing fountain become a place for God's presence as an eternal well to those who come to drink in the spiritual blessings it offers. It brings regeneration to the thirsty and struggling lives that come for a touch of God to help them. The chapel is a setting that people can come to even though God can minister to them anywhere they call upon him in prayer. The sick find it a place to run to for God's help. Doctors know patients look for places to turn to, including home remedies, herbal and nutritional programs, and other places for additional remedies, They seem to find comfort in a place to go for help.

The apostle Paul's prayerful blessing for the Thessalonians he had ministered to was:

> *Now may the God of peace Himself sanctify you completely; and may your whole spirit, soul, and body be preserved blameless at the coming of our Lord Jesus Christ* (1 Thessalonians 5:23).

He desired that their whole being would be yielded to the will of God. The power of this accomplishment comes directly from the God of peace, which is what we all long for in our inner beings. God's faithfulness is that He will do it for us if we yield ourselves to Him. No matter our past beliefs, transgressions, or experiences, to come to His healing waters is to come to His redeeming heart and receive His gift of grace and mercy. He longs for us to come to Him for fullness of healing of our body, soul, and spirit. He revives and regenerates our weary spirits, bringing life and strength to our bodies.

Place of Restoration

The Holy Spirit is the agent of restoration. As He pours out His Spirit on all people, we sit quietly worshiping in the presence of God. The Spirit fills us with the supernatural works of God to be done through us. He even brings salvation and regeneration of the dry spirit of humankind with cleansing, making the new man acceptable to God; this is the work of the Holy Spirit. (See Joel 2:18-27.) Then, His Word declares that they will be empowered to witness of Him, and their witness will spread the good news throughout the world. Healed and restored lives will become living witnesses to the world. The Lord Jesus is your life, and He has come to bring life abundantly. Believing in him releases the power of God. All this can happen at the wellspring in the medical center or wherever God's people gather to worship Him and call upon Him in their time of need. He revives the weary hearts of the people. He brings a taste of Heaven out of His heart for the people coming to Him.

Fueled by Father God's Love

The heart of the Father's love is at the core of this ministry. It is His heart for our healing, freedom, and justice for all. His Father's heart heals the depressed or oppressed heart. In the well of His presence, the concerns of the world seem to fade to lesser importance as we bask in the Father's love. We learn to know the sound of His beating heart, established for Kingdom purposes in our lives. All may enter His presence for freedom and liberty from the crippling effects of illness. We want to shout to all the invitation to "Come!" The healing and restoration is deep. It takes us beyond the healing need and awakens us to be free to fulfill destiny in life.

> *One thing I ask of the Lord, this is what I seek: that I may dwell in the house of the Lord all the days of my life.... Hear my voice when I call, O Lord; be merciful to me and answer me.... Do not reject me or forsake me, O God my Savior.... Teach me Your way, O Lord; lead me in a straight path.... I am still confident of this: I will see the goodness of the Lord in the land of the living* (Psalms 27:4,7,9,11,13 NIV).

Here is a place to experience the Lord. Taste and see the goodness of the Lord in this place of refuge.

How It All Began

I first got interested in opening a healing prayer service at the Penn State Hershey Medical Center after reading Cal Pierce's book, *Preparing the Way*.[2] It is about healing evangelist John G. Lake, who opened healing rooms in Spokane, Washington, in 1914, because he had a burden for the sick in America. He put together a healing team and rented rooms in an office building. They gained 100,000 documented healings, and the federal government declared it "the healthiest city in the world." Officials in Deaconess Medical Center in Spokane noticed that they had a lack of patients, because patients had a healthcare choice in Spokane. If they were sick, they could go to the hospital or have alternative healing by a healing prayer team.

Cal Pierce went to "re-dig" those healing wells of revival and bring them to do the same healings in his new healing rooms. He reopened the historic healing ministry of pioneer John G. Lake's healing rooms for physical and emotional healings. They were manned by volunteers from surrounding churches. Counselors were trained to receive the presence of the Holy Spirit and have humility and unity as they ministered God's healing anointing to the patients. They found water in Medical Lake in Spokane that seemed to carry a healing anointing like the pools of Bethesda (meaning "house of mercy") where people got healed. They kept a vase of the miracle healing waters in the healing rooms.

As Cal Pierce went to re-dig the healing wells from John G. Lake's healing rooms, he would toss out the doubt and unbelief that clogged the spiritual wells. And he vowed to believe God that He would come again to bring those healings. He gave training to his healing prayer ministers in which they studied the spiritual authority they had as believers to heal. The authority is to break the yoke of affliction and bring the glory of the Lord to the lives of the sick.

A friend of mine told me the Lord showed her He wanted to establish His prayer altar in the Hershey Medical Center. Being a former behavioral science professor at the Hershey Medical Center, I had a heart to see that fulfilled. After we prayed about it for a while, I sensed it was time for us to open a healing ministry in the Medical Center chapel. Cal Pierce had begun a healing-room movement, and they were opening around the world. However, I believed we needed to have healing prayer right in the hospital where the sick were being treated, and the healing ministry needed to be structured a bit differently to work well in the medical setting. God also showed that other faiths were using the interfaith prayer chapel as their prayer altar, and He wanted us to use it as His prayer altar.

In 2003, we started praying about it. We took a team into the Medical Center for a prayer walk to discern the best way and place to do it. As soon as we got near the interfaith chapel, we got introduced to the head chaplain, who took us into his conference room and asked what we wanted to do. When we said we wanted to have an ecumenical Christian prayer time with prayer ministers from various regional churches, he was very interested in helping us establish that ministry.

Soon, we were trained as official hospital pastoral care volunteers and we did our own healing ministry training that could be done in the Medical Center setting, and we began our weekly prayer ministry. The chaplain taught us the political nuances that needed to be heeded in the hospital setting, and we began our ministry there. The chaplain warned us not to evangelize or to go pray over people that did not ask for it. He advised us to let patients come to us in the chapel, and then we could be free in offering Christian healing prayers.

We set our prayer service before the Muslim weekly service so we could offer them healing prayers as well. We did have some Muslims come into our prayer time and receive Jesus' healing prayers. They told us *that* the Qur'an speaks more of Jesus and His ministry on earth than it speaks about Allah. They were very aware of Jesus' healing ministry and openly received our healing prayers. They appealed to us to have a peaceable relationship being there together, and we agreed we would focus on the things that we agreed upon. It was surprising to us to find they did believe Jesus had many healings and miracles when He walked the earth, and they would receive a Jesus prayer for healing.

A Muslim man who had chronic headaches for years allowed us to pray for him and bless him. And when his headache left, he wondered how we did it. When he realized God answered our prayers, he noted that we had an unusual blessing of God with us. He continued to come to our prayer time before his and asked for prayer for other concerns as well. They showed us their black seed oil that they believe heals anything but death. But we showed them our healing balm of Gilead that heals everything, including bringing life over death, because of the resurrection power of Jesus. We educated each other on our faiths, and they were impressed by the "alive spirit" in our prayer time. They also noted that our God heard and answered our prayers. Some weeks they would come early and see the ministry happening to the families of the sick. They watched intently, as our prayer service is very different from theirs, with a strong presence of a God who listens and ministers to our needs.

A Muslim woman went to her prayer corner while we were having our prayer time. A man came in to praise God for his healing he received at our last prayer service. Then another woman came to thank God. The Muslim woman heard the rejoicing in our prayer time and was amazed at how we rejoice and thank God in our prayers. She enjoyed seeing that and wanted to see more of what God was doing in our prayer service. I asked her if she had a prayer request, and she did have one for her husband. She told us he needed a job, so we said we would pray. The next week she came back and exclaimed that her husband got his job and God heard our prayers. Again, people came in to thank God for healings while she listened. She was so struck she came in with a girlfriend the next week to say how wonderful our prayers were.

God's Redemptive Healing Love

The Penn State Hershey Medical Center was first built with $50 million from the trust of Milton S. Hershey, the man who built the town, the chocolate factory, and the school for orphans. His business prospered, as he had a heart to take in the orphans to give them a better life. He built the first hospital in the town and wanted it to be a research hospital because his own wife had a progressive muscular disease that doctors had not yet diagnosed. When Milton was treated for heart problems himself, doctors noted that he had the largest physical heart they had ever seen.

This man also had a big heart for the community and a big heart to care for the orphans of the community. He carried the heart of Father God for all people and built the town to meet all the needs of the community. Milton's heart, which had been nurtured by his Mennonite mother's simple faith, reflected God's heart for healing and redemption. It was a heart to take orphans into homes with house parents to guide them and to meet their every need, and to have them and the chocolate worker families so satisfied in the town that they would not need to leave.

Place of Healing and Redemption

At the Penn State Hershey Medical Center, healing and redemption come to those coming for God's help as God's people display the kind of love Jesus demonstrated as He walked the earth and healed them during His earthly ministry. By His love He said all people would know His disciples. God's refreshing, restoring love is what compelled Him to heal and speak edifying words to the people. His redemptive love restores heart and soul by the Spirit of God that fills the medical center chapel as a spiritual house inhabited by believing ministers, so that all men would be drawn unto Him. The Spirit of God is flowing in the refreshing fountain atmosphere in the chapel to beckon all people to come: *"God is our refuge and strength, a very present help in trouble"* (Ps. 46:1).

No matter what comes we will not fear, though the waters roar and be troubled.

There is a river whose streams shall make glad the city of God, the holy place of the tabernacle of the Most High. God is in the midst of her, she shall not be moved... (Psalms 46:4-5).

No matter what storms are in our lives, the refuge of the Lord in the chapel is symbolic of the refuge we have in God no matter what storms come. Even if wars rage among the nations the Lord is with us, and we can come to Him to care for our body and soul at the well of His presence wherever we find a refuge of strength for our souls.

The story of Hagar sitting by the well but dying of thirst is an interesting one. Having run from Abraham and Sarah's household into the desert with her son Ishmael, and having come to a place where she sat believing she and her son were dying of thirst, she cries out to God. She says, "God, don't let me see my son die," and suddenly God, hearing her prayer, opens her eyes and she sees a stream of living water bubbling out of the ground right next to her (see Gen. 21:15-19). Suddenly, after crying out to God for help, she realizes His provision, and her life was rescued. God showed her He was with her as she cried out to Him, though she didn't realize it until He opened her eyes to it.

Place of Refreshment

The Penn State Hershey Medical Center healing service prayer team sustains each one as they come for spiritual refreshment. Some come in just looking for a place to sit and rest. And then they are surprised to find their eyes open to greater sustaining help from God's healing ministers.

Elijah also found himself hiding for safety and lying by the brook, Kerith, during a drought in Israel that he had prophesied to the people. He told the worshipers of Baal, who believed that their god controlled the weather, that God would bring a drought (see 1 Kings 17:1-6). God provided a living stream for Elijah, with ravens bringing the food he needed to sustain his life in the drought. In First Kings 17, when the brook ran dry God sent him to a widow who needed food and oil for her household. Elijah did his first miracle for her, providing the sustenance she needed—enough oil for the rest of the drought (see 1 Kings 17:7-24). God did His reviving work in Elijah and then through him to pour out miracles. He restores us first by the wellspring and then uses us to pour out healing miracles into the lives of others. In our pouring out to others, God pours back into us, filling our needs as we fill the needs of others.

God's Seed of a Nation Brings Healing

There is a historic seed of a nation being watered at this medical center. It is no surprise this healing center would be in Pennsylvania, at the Penn State Hershey Medical Center. The land was granted to William Penn after he was set free from the Tower of London, where he was a prisoner of conscience. He believed God wanted healing freedom for people in every sense. Penn believed his God would make Pennsylvania the Seed of a Nation, be a holy example for the nations. Here in this land of Penn's holy experiment, we find Penn State Hershey Medical Center becoming a model for healing that other hospitals want to emulate. It is a university hospital with the best of science and the best of unified prayer for healing that could make a great impact as a model of the best coming together. There is a historical medical precedent in Pennsylvania since Benjamin Franklin opened the first American Medical School and Hospital in Philadelphia in 1765.

Once people believe in God's healing faith grows in the hearts of the people—it nurtures the seed until the healing result is seen. In our bodies, it is happening on a cellular level until it becomes measurable. Once the words of God are spoken and believed, healing Scriptures take root in the heart of man, and a model of new life springs forth.

Stories Drawing People's Hearts

This kind of ministry in the community is Christianity in operation as good news today. This is church people being relevant to the needs of the community. Hosting a chapel prayer service in a medical center provides a place of holy habitation for the Lord God to minister His presence to those in need. The Lord summons people in the busyness of their lives with the distresses of life in the balance, finances in the balance, and concerns for loved ones. The Lord draws their spirits. He speaks: "Come to Me, all who are weary, and I will give you rest. Come, can you feel My arms around you? My eyes are upon you. Can you feel My pleasure over you, my precious ones? *Even in the midst of your distresses, feel My spirit ministering to you. I am in the midst of your situation. This is Christianity today.* I *am* dwelling with you. Feel My compassion for you. Know that I am good. Feel My joy over you."

Two families came into the chapel at the same time. This was a wife and daughter having to decide whether to pull the plug on her husband. She was desperately asking the Lord for wisdom and strength to know what to do, trusting that the Lord had her in His hands, but not wanting to have the weight of a decision to end a life on her shoulders. The team surrounding her had a sense of peace as she sat encircled by prayer ministers. She knew the Lord was good, and she had a peace that it was in His hands as the team supported her prayers before the throne of God.

While she was in the chapel, two sisters also came to pray for their mother, who had an out-of-control bacterial infection. They said they knew their lives would bring them to this moment. Their mother had been resuscitated twice the day before and was still in a coma. They declared their peace before God, feeling the pain, but feeling the Lord's comfort and the prayer team's support. Even in their pain, they turned to pray for the woman making the decision for her husband's life. They supported each other and went back to the ICU having a spirit-bond to support each other in their crises of life. Both families left the altar with an inner sense of peace, committing their loved ones into the Lord's hands and knowing He would be faithful to them. This kind of ministry—one to another even in the midst of suffering and grief—is a welcome joy to give and receive help from one another, understanding what each other is experiencing.

Another woman was dying of cancer and asked for our team to come to her room. Doctors didn't expect her to live through the night. But she revived after receiving the prayer and lived for a few weeks for our prayer team visits. She confided in us that she wanted to marry her live-in boyfriend. Even though she had end-stage cancer and her life was in the balance, she wanted to make things right with God. She wanted a clear conscience and prayed to be able to make things right even at the end of her life. After things were cleared in her spirit, she had a peace to let go and passed into eternity as a woman right with God. Hers was a life redeemed through her trial with cancer.

Another young man fell off a balcony, partying and drinking. He hit his head and broke his back. Doctors decided not to fix his injured shoulder because they didn't expect him to ever wake up from a coma. But believing prayers surrounded his bedside, and he woke up. Soon, he recovered enough that he was transferred to rehabilitation. His troubled life was saved by the Lord. He and his wife increased in faith. Soon, he got the faith to walk, though doctors said he never would walk. He showed up in church in a wheelchair, and part of our team picked him up to stand for the first time. Next he was walking in rehabilitation. The Lord cheered him on with a prayer team coaching and supporting his strength of faith to beat the odds.

Another patient had a massive stroke and was in a coma when his wife asked for prayer, saying their marriage was strained, but praying he would be healed. He woke up from the coma and said he heard bells ringing and saw Jesus. Jesus gave him peace in the vision and a second chance at life. He woke up from the coma wanting to be a better man, and he wanted to know how to get back to Jesus as a believer on Earth and live a better life. This revived their marriage and his zeal for life. His left side had been fully paralyzed, but movement was restored enough for him to get around with a slight limp, which reminded him of his new Savior.

Chapel Prayer for Medical Staff Needs

The prayer chapel also became a place for medical staff to come and share their need for wisdom and help for patients in their care. The chapel is a place of peace and rest for medical staff who need it, too. They find a quick respite in the midst of busy schedules and serious decisions to make over families in trauma. They find personal relief to have prayer support as they ask for the Lord's help, especially for difficult cases.

When an Amish school shooting brought some of the ten girls shot to the medical center, it became an overwhelming grief not only to the families but to the medical and pastoral care staff as well. The tragic trauma to such pure young girls in faithful families in the Amish community was more than people could bear. Though the Amish wanted to keep it private and close in their family support, the team still prayed for them and for staff. We prayed with school girl friends and boyfriends who cared so much for the girls they wanted to take the burden on themselves. Some went before God in their barns to intercede for their friends.

The chapel is a place of God's presence to heal emotions as people cry out to God and find, not an empty chapel, but a chapel filled with love and support. We say, "Come!" The Spirit and the Bride of Christ say come in the chapel. Let Your presence, Lord, dwell among us in the midst of our trauma and make it well with our souls.

Ministering to the Lord

We delight in ministering to the Lord as inner-court ministry when only the prayer team is in the chapel. We pray for the guardian and healing angels of the Lord to move around the medical center and minister to each one in their rooms. We call upon the Lord to draw near to their bedsides and minister in a way that they know the Lord is with them. Some patients have told us they sense an angel in their rooms, coming to minister to them and bring healing to their bodies. Some medical staff tell us they stand at the nurses' desks in the center of the units discussing God stories of what the Lord has done to enhance the medical care and minister healing to the patients.

We know the Lord wants to help all people, but His heart is especially for restoring destinies of children when they have dire diagnoses. We pray their names and the meanings of their names, calling forth destinies in how their parents were moved to name them and see vision over their lives. We agree with the parents as they cry out for their children's lives.

Some are rescued with healing and some aren't. It is hard to comprehend how some receive new life on earth and some pass on. But the Lord strengthens the families as they come to Him in the chapel, and He shows His goodness even in the midst of grief.

Amazingly, families still come to thank us for showing the Lord's loving pursuit of them in their time of need. Even some who lose their children still come back feeling a bond with us for standing with them when they brought their children before the Lord. It is a sweet memory to hold onto that the Kingdom of God is near when He heals, and even when they pass into eternity. Romans states, *"...the sufferings of this present time are not worthy to be compared with the glory which shall be revealed in us"* (Rom. 8:18).

Truly, people in their tragedy see the enduring love of God giving an inner comfort and peace when there are no comforting words a person could speak like the Holy Spirit speaks. They know His presence and love that endures forever as an inner contentment as they feel the prayers and faithfulness of God in their midst. The anointing of the Lord that was on Jesus to redeem everyone that came to Him for help is upon a chapel ministry that comes to the altar of the Lord to be a place of refuge and strength—a strong tower for all to run into when their hearts and souls so desperately need it.

Shalom in the Chapel

The chapel ministry is for all to come, no matter what their life or health issues have been. When they come to Jesus, His grace and mercy soothes their heart cry. *Like the Father God who comes and comforts us and says, "Everything will be OK,"* people can walk out saying, "It is well with my soul."

Stoking the altar with prayer from week to week brings the presence of the spirit of God who ministers to needy people and brings a peace that rests in the atmosphere. The faithful prayers at the altar in the medical center seem to increase the anointing of peace in that place. People comment as they walk into the chapel that they sense a peaceful presence of God as they come in. The sweet words spoken to people become life-giving words to minister healing love to their souls, restoring life and faith. God is in the business of restoring souls at His prayer altar before Him.

Faith is Strengthened

The fruit that comes forth is the strength of testimonies of what the Lord has done that goes back to revive families. Where faith was lost, people's faith is strengthened. And testimonies of what the Lord has done become testimonies that the Lord can repeat as people who have overcome sickness and death come to pray for others facing the same thing, saying, "Lord do it again for this one!" This is the surprising love of God to many who don't know Him in the medical setting. People are surprised to come into the hospital and find prayer ministers to meet them in their time of need. They are so moved to find that support that they come back even after discharge to say thank you to God and to the team.

They find God to have a greater love than they ever knew as they find His support in their time of need. Where could they go? Where could they find His love when they might not be churchgoers? It surprises them and moves them to tears, giving them new ideas about how to pray and how to find strength in prayer. It draws them to want more of God, if He is this loving God who cares about their personal lives and needs. This is the God of Christianity today that draws people to His loving care.

This is the God that the world craves in their hearts as they are concerned about wars and rumors of wars, about potential attacks and natural disasters, about viruses and plagues. This is the God they can run to who meets us at our point of need. Sometimes He brings a miraculous story. But more often He brings His healing comfort to our weary souls.

True Rest for Weary Souls

Jesus gives true rest. Religious leaders of His day found fault in His healing on the Sabbath and His quiet claim that He was the Son of God and could forgive the sins of the world. Though the religious leaders had a growing opposition to His healings, His disciples continued to go about meeting human needs. Though they claimed His healing power was not of God, He and His disciples went about quietly meeting the needs of everyone who came to Him. Though the wise and prudent didn't see His goodness, the weary and sick benefited by His care. He called out, *"Come to Me, all you who labor and are heavy laden, and I will give you rest"* (Matt. 11:28). He strengthened the weary and downhearted. He strengthened them saying, *"Take My yoke upon you and learn from Me, for I am gentle and lowly in heart, and you will find rest for your souls"* (Matt. 11:29).

Take His yoke upon you and find rest for your souls! Through this ministry, many will see and hear by experience that He is God. Many will come to know God as He causes the deepest ministry to bless *their hearts.*

My Yoke is Easy

You will display His glory as you bring your burden to Him, and you will find the burden is light because He carries the weight of the burden as we walk alongside, yoked to Him, like an ox walking yoked to another ox that shares the load. The burden is actually pleasant and comfortable because it is connected with God and His leadership over it. With Him, our sicknesses and sufferings don't seem so overwhelming. In fact, if we look to Him to lead us through it we can trust Him and make it through.

The revelation He brings as we yield to Him opens us up to new realms of faith in the midst of the storms of life. Faith lifts us up to not lose hope but to keep vision and strength to sustain us through the storms. Yoked with God, the storms don't seem so frightening, because we know it is in His hands and He is leading us through it. We move to higher levels of faith that sustain us and give God's perspective. He gives a spirit of wisdom and revelation, and we gain a peace beyond human understanding (see Eph. 1:17). We gain peace because the Spirit of Peace sustains us. We receive spiritual understanding and the spiritual fruit of peace, love, joy, longsuffering, and patience that sustains us in a glorious way even if we have to face death.

I was with my father in his last days of struggling with life. He got so weak he couldn't eat or talk and seemed to be in a sleep-state. When I knew the time was near I told him how much I appreciated him and his life well lived. And I told him I loved him. Somehow, though he seemed asleep, he mouthed the words, "I love you, too." That moment brought a lasting peace between us, though I knew he was dying. When he got to his last breath I thought I would be sad, but I had such a sense of joy as I saw him peacefully pass that I was overwhelmed with the thought that his was a life well lived and he had finished his race in life and won his victory to be with his Jesus. So the moment of death became a moment of joy and victory, seeing it from God's perspective. In the Lord's grace, He gave every member of our family a sweet time with Dad before he passed. The Lord led us through that time of suffering and bore for us the sting of death.

"Comfort, comfort My people, says your God" (Isa. 40:1 NIV). The Holy Spirit calls Himself the Holy Comforter who will comfort us in our time of need that we might know His comfort and be able to give to others what we have received from Him. I remember the overwhelming grief I felt when my 40-year-old brother suddenly died of a heart attack, but the Lord used the truth of a verse to comfort my soul when I was crying out to Him, not understanding why He would allow my brother to die in the prime of his life. I opened my Bible to study the book of Nehemiah, and my spirit lighted on Nehemiah's words to the people of Israel: *"Do not sorrow, for the joy of the Lord is your strength"* (Neh. 8:10). Those words sunk into my spirit, and the Lord lifted my grief to become a sense of the joy of the Lord as an inner strength inside me. The word was a healing balm that lifted the overwhelming grief in my heart to be able to go on in the strength of the Lord.

Jesus' Love Fills the Chapel

Each week in the chapel we begin with worship and prayer and wait for God's presence to come to minister to the people. We pursue Him and pray cleansing prayers that nothing would hinder the flow of His presence. He seems to give us a time of quiet worship before Him. As we sit before Him with listening prayer and quiet worship, we wait to see the needs in the people He brings for that day. Each week He tends to bring themes of needs and prayers. One week everyone that came to the chapel had needs for lungs. We prayed for the spirit of life to fill their lungs and push out any cancer that hindered breathing. We prayed for His Spirit to blow over the needs in the chapel; we remembered how He breathed life into Adam and how He restores life with the breath of His Spirit.

Another week the theme was burn patients. A man came in asking if we would baptize him. He had been burned and his legs injured in an accident, and the trauma made him realize God had spared him from death. He wanted to get right with God, so he wanted to be baptized in the hospital chapel before he was discharged. We sprinkled water on him from the fountain and baptized him. Then we found out he was a firefighter and God wanted to baptize the chapel with the fire of His presence. So the team got a blessing back from the man who wanted baptism.

Another week we had back patients. One man needed back surgery but wanted God's prayers not to have the surgery. We prayed for alignment of his back, and he came several weeks in a row wanting healing prayer to get his back in alignment. As we prayed he wanted more things in alignment. He ended up not needing the surgery!

The spiritual atmosphere created in the chapel lifts people from discouragement and resignation to the sickness and suffering and fears of the worst with medical diagnoses and the risks involved. But the chapel atmosphere is one of hope and trust in God that encourages people and gives them new perspective to call upon God's help in their time of trouble.

Faith rises as people realize: *"Now faith is being sure of what we hope for and certain of what we do not see"* (Heb. 11:1 NIV). We rely on the Word of God and ask God to fulfill His words to us. And the God of hope fills us with joy and peace as our trust levels rise in Him (see Rom. 15:13).

Resurrection Glory

> *...the Father of Glory, may give to you the spirit of wisdom and revelation in the knowledge of Him...and what is the exceeding greatness of His power toward us who believe, according to the working of His mighty power* (Ephesians 1:17,19).

God will release not only healing power but also revelation to know His purposes. God is revealing resurrection knowledge in these days so believers will know His power and works.[3] Both Elijah and Elisha raised the dead, and we can learn from what they did.

> *He stretched himself out on the child three times, and cried out to the Lord and said, "O Lord my God, I pray, let this child's soul come back to him"* (1 Kings 17:21).

Then the Lord heard the voice of Elijah, and the soul of the child came back to him. Elisha did a similar thing in Second Kings. He lay on the child, put his mouth on his mouth, his eyes on his eyes, and his hands on his hands, and stretched himself out on the child, and the child became warm, sneezed seven times, and opened his eyes (see 2 Kings 4:34-35). This is the origination of mouth-to-mouth resuscitation, used in crisis medical care today. Just as God breathed life into Adam, so did Elisha breathe life into the child.

A Muslim girl from Uzbekistan became a Christian and was endangered. She leaned against a wall where there was a bomb that exploded at the back of her head. Her body was burned and her head blown open. She died, and her soul went to Heaven. She saw Jesus, and He welcomed her and asked her if she wanted to stay. This was happening while her family was praying desperately for her life. She told Jesus she wanted another chance to go back and tell people about Him. Then she woke up in her body, and her body began to heal. Today she has only a scar in her head. No other scars are visible on her body. God gave her a miraculous testimony to build other people's faith.

He speaks: *"I have loved you with an everlasting love; you have captured My heart. I have seen you as you truly are. I have heard your cries to Me; I will show you great things to come. Come to Me. Sit awhile in My presence. Know your loved ones are in My hand. Know your concerns are in My hand. See Me as I see you!"* Jesus gives *true rest* to our souls. Jesus says, *"Don't carry the burden of legalism. Have an open, free relationship with Me. I will take your burdens, your sickness."* This is Christianity *today*. Not religion, but relationship with Jesus.

Healing Revival Wellspring

Having prayed for healing life to be revived in the chapel, for five years we have prayerfully dug deep into the historical wells that existed in the land and in the heart of God. There are wells of healing and revival from the days of William Penn, from the Quakers and their efforts to set slaves free; from the Anabaptist, peace-making simple faith there is wisdom and steadfast love of God over the years. Entrepreneurial wells of Milton Hershey's chocolate making and orphan care. Wells of healing as Milton Hershey searched for the best doctors and researchers to care for his wife and community friends. Prayers that converge together and stir the heart of God in the heavenlies.

Prayers that cry out for healing and Father love have been heard at the well of His presence. They had dug deep as teams from different churches and streams of different denominations come together with believing prayer. All come to find breakthrough and God's healing help. Everyday wisdom balanced with spiritual perspective brings practical guidance for how to live in perfect peace with God and fellow human beings.

The invitation goes out through those who have been there and want to share the blessings. "Come to find Jesus." All who are thirsty, the Lord will give you rest for your heart's cry. Patients come for this wisdom. So do doctors! Everyone has that deep heart's cry to come to the living God and find healing and direction to answer life's questions. Come to the well, dig deep in the spirit of prayer, and find the flow of the Spirit and the Word of God that springs forth for you.

Endnotes

1. Mark D. Siljander, *A Deadly Misunderstanding: A Congressman's Quest to Bridge the Muslim-Christian Divide* (New York: HarperOne, 2008).

2. Cal Pierce, *Preparing the Way* (Hagerstown, MD: McDougal Publishers, 2001), 11.

3. David Herzog, *Glory Invasion* (Shippensburg, PA: Destiny Image Publishers, 2007).

Chapter 2

God's Original Design for Healing

...I am the Lord who heals you (Exodus 15:26).

God identifies Himself to the Israelites as the Great Physician, saying, *"I am the Lord who heals you."* This is a redemptive name He gives Himself. He later displayed His healing love through the ministry of Jesus Christ and through the apostles, demonstrating that He truly is their redeemer. When Jesus was preparing to leave the earth He said we could do even greater things than He did (see John 14:12). Malachi 4 declares, "He will arise with healing in his wings." He carries the resurrection power for our healing.

God established a healing covenantal theme for His people throughout history and throughout His revealed Word. It first comes as the Israelites are escaping the oppressive rule of the Egyptian pharaoh. They have seen the plagues even unto death that God sent to convince Pharaoh that he must let the Israelites go free. They saw Moses ask Pharaoh for freedom, but Pharaoh denied it until God sent too many plagues. After his own son's death, Pharaoh became desperate to finally release them to leave Egypt. They saw the hand of the Lord miraculously part the Red Sea on their behalf, stopping the oppressive pharaoh and allowing the Israelites to run safely to their promised land where God would dwell with them. In the Lord's mercy, He led forth His people to be redeemed from oppression and led them to His holy habitation in the Promised Land. Rejoicing in this great victory, yet bitterly complaining that they had no clean water to drink in the desert, God presents them with a covenantal life lesson that will guide them for all time. He declares himself *Jehovah Rapha*, saying, *"I am the God who heals you."* And these are the covenantal conditions they will understand from what He just showed them in their journey to freedom. Here begins the covenant and three principles God declares regarding healing in His Word:

1. *"I am the Lord who heals you"* (Exod. 15:26).
2. *"The prayer of faith will save the sick, and the Lord will raise him up..."* (James 5:15).
3. *"Jesus Christ is the same yesterday, today, and forever"* (Heb. 13:8). *"I am the Lord, I change not..."* (Mal. 3:6 KJV).

God created us in His image for fellowship with Him and will go to lavish extents to redeem us back to Himself and His holy purposes. He brought Jesus to earth to be the saving grace for our healing and used His teachings and healings to confirm His personal loving care for His people. Jesus' healings demonstrated the power of His love and the authority of His Kingdom on earth. But God's ultimate goal is that we would be a healed people who love Him and fulfill His purposes to bring His Kingdom to the earth. *Healing has a greater purpose than bodily health. It is for wholeness and freedom to have dominion over the earth as He intended.* He is the Lord who heals us, but healing is the fruit of His holy purposes and His love for his people.

Theology of Suffering Helps Healing

A principle many of us have trouble understanding with our earthly minds is why God would allow us to suffer and who caused it in the first place. Job's greatest suffering was at the thought of why God would allow it. His friends caused him distress in their counsel, telling him to look at what he had done wrong to have gotten these sufferings. People struggle to find meaning in the suffering, and their suffering is increased if they think guilt or shame is the reason they have the sickness. Even the disciples tried to understand this as they asked Jesus, *"Rabbi, who sinned, this man or his parents, that he was born blind?"* (John 9:2). The disciples believed suffering was the result of sin, but Jesus' response was not to point the finger in judgment toward anyone. His response was that there is a greater glory perspective in the blind man's testimony. Jesus responded, *"Neither this man nor his parents sinned, but that the works of God should be revealed in him"* (John 9:3).

In Jesus' hands, the man's blindness was to manifest the wonder-working power of God. Could it be that God allowed us to be wounded so that He might heal us and bring glory to our lives? This is a principle we have trouble comprehending— that God would permit a wounding into our lives for a greater healing purpose. Martha didn't understand why Jesus wouldn't come when her brother was dying, but He tarried intentionally to demonstrate His resurrection power in Lazarus' life. We don't understand why God uses suffering until we experience what it does in our lives by going through it.

Shepherds demonstrate an important lesson in this principle. A shepherd would break the leg of a lamb that was going astray so he could carry the lamb and hold it close to his heart while the leg heals. Then, when the lamb could walk again, he wouldn't stray from the shepherd because his heart had become close to the shepherd's heart and he wouldn't want to leave the shepherd's side. This is similar to Jesus being the wounded Healer who understands our heart after experiencing suffering Himself. We help one another through what we learn in overcoming our sufferings.

Romans states: *"For I consider that the sufferings of this present time are not worthy to be compared with the glory which shall be revealed in us"* (Rom. 8:18). This passage became dear to me when my young cousin was dying of painful skin cancer. The Lord said the glory in him would be stronger than the suffering he went through. He sang a solo in the Easter musical months before he died. The song was "He's Alive." The congregation was moved by the message of the song being sung so powerfully through a young man dying himself. Yet his eyes sparkled with the message—*He's Alive!*

We see this in operation when we see people come into the medical center chapel to pray for their own health or that of their loved ones. As they come into the meditative worship atmosphere and find prayer ministers to minister to them, they often are moved to tears at the loving concern God has for their suffering. It moves them to share family concerns beyond the healing need. They talk about things that need to be straightened out in their family relationships and family members that might have strayed like prodigal children. They want help for healing, but they also open up to share so many more needs to get their family at peace with God and His purposes in their lives.

The Healing Covenant

This God who is the same yesterday, today, and forevermore told the Israelites, *"I am the Lord who heals you"* (Exod. 15:26). The prayer of faith in Him makes the sick person well (see James 5:15 NIV). Moses tells of the Lord's sovereignty:

> *You in Your mercy have led forth the people whom You
> have redeemed; You have guided them in Your strength to
> Your holy habitation* (Exodus 15:13).

Then they came to Marah. They could not drink the waters
of Marah for they were bitter. Then Moses threw a *tree* into the
waters. When he cast it into the waters they were made sweet—
healing waters were released. Then he made a statute and an or-
dinance and tested them.

> *"If you diligently heed the voice of the Lord your God and do
> what is right in His sight, give ear to His commandments
> and keep all His statutes, I will put none of the diseases on
> you which I have brought on the Egyptians. **For I am the
> Lord who heals you.**" Then they came to Elim, where there
> were twelve wells of water and seventy palm trees; so they
> camped there by the waters* (Exodus 15:26-27).

There were bitter wells and pools in this region that were often
brackish. This was a representation of the spirits of the people
that were bitter toward Moses, their leader, and toward God, even
though three days before that they experienced the Red Sea miraculous rescue. There were many occasions when the people had
bitter heart responses to their conditions, even though God was
miraculously freeing them from the Egyptian bondage. But God
had a cure for the bitter waters and the bitter people. "*... The Lord
showed him a tree. When he cast it into the waters, the waters were
made sweet*" (Exod. 15:25). Jesus died on a tree—the Cross—to
redeem us from the bitterness. This is a covenant God is establishing with a condition on our part. We must purify the bitter
waters to purify our bitter heart reaction to life's distresses. Just as
the waters needed healing, so the people's hearts needed to be set
free from bitterness. The Cross is symbolic of the tree tossed in
the bitter waters to purify them and let a pure river of life flow for
the people! By Jesus' stripes we are healed. By the bitter lashing

of angry hearts filled with hatred against Jesus, our Redeemer, we are set free. Jesus' shed blood provides our atonement for sin. This is the divine healing covenant.

The Cross enables us to make the choice to heed His voice and it provides for us to receive the healing grace. He wants us to heed his voice, yet he heals even those who don't obey, which is a demonstration of his saving grace, and often has that impact in their lives. God declared Himself *Jehovah Rapha*, the God who heals. *"I am the Lord who heals you."* He is the Great Physician with the greatest healing remedy. This verse speaks of physical diseases and divine cures.

Abraham prayed to God to heal Abimelech's household so they could bear children after God had closed the wombs of his household because of Sarah, Abraham's wife (see Gen. 20:17). God responded and opened their wombs. And God brought remedies for cures from leprosy and boils. He gave the prescription to the priests to examine sick people and treat them with personal and social hygiene, protecting the community by isolating them. And the priests could pray for healing and declare them healed with a special sacrificial purifying ritual (see Lev. 14:3-7). The healing prescription was written out by God to be implemented through the priests to heal the sick and protect the community from the spread of sickness.

The divine healing covenant is to keep nations free from diseases under the condition of diligent obedience to personal spiritual and physical purity. This is a lifestyle of living right before God and having peace in body, soul, and spirit. His very name declares His ability to pronounce health and restore as we obey His healing prescription in His Word. *We can recover health and sustain health as we walk in His divine law of purity and love.* Though sin and disobedience are not always the direct cause of sickness, humanity's fall into sin is the original and underlying cause of disease. We can seek healing by looking to Christ, our Redeemer and our sin-bearer, and pursuing His consecration. And because he bore our sin for us, God brings grace to us even on this healing covenant.

The healing covenant was established with a nation of people—the Israelites. God had a prescription for all to be well, for all to come back to fellowship with Him and one another and enjoy wholeness and health. He intended us to live in health and fulfill our purposes. He wants us to get over our sicknesses and be restored to fellowship with Him and with others so we can prosper in the land of the living.

The book of Deuteronomy, the book of the law, calls us to love the Lord our God and find prosperity in all that we set our hand to do. He set a godly order in our lives to love the Lord first. He brings divine order and divine health.

God's Redemptive Health Principles

Principles for healthful living are listed in detail in the Holy Scriptures. But the ultimate health is seen in the apostle's prayer, *"Beloved, I pray that you may prosper in all things and be in health, just as your soul prospers"* (3 John 1:2). Health and healing are means God uses to get our attention to realize the authority of His Kingdom coming in our lives. It puts a holy fear in us of His personal care over our lives. But His ultimate purpose for us is to live in heath and focus our energy, not on healing, but on fulfilling God's purposes in our lives.

When God declared His name to be Rapha, He was revealing the part of His character that cures, heals, repairs, mends, and restores. It happened for many people at a well. The Samaritan woman found new life at a well when Jesus spoke living words over her life. It happened when Rebecca was found for

Isaac at a well. It happened when Naaman was cleansed in water seven times and healed, and it happened for the paralytic man at the Gate Beautiful. Wells and palm trees were the sustenance of life. Deborah sat by a palm tree and shared her wisdom as a judge. As the people first came to 12 wells of water and 70 palm trees, refreshing springs of water for the 12 tribes were released. Each family had its healing well. Their palm trees provided the covering and refreshing shade to rest in as they were refreshed. Though they were slaves in Egypt, they were now being set free and refreshed by pure wells of healing water. And a key element in the purity for healing was to release them from bitterness that lowered their immunity to sickness.

We are called to *"...Dwell in the land, and feed on His faithfulness"* (Ps. 37:3). We are called to find healing communion with God like Adam and Eve first had in the Garden. Eve's deception, which undermined God's word of life forevermore to her, brought separation of that communion with God and resulted in death and strife. But God intended full communion in the Garden and wants to restore us to that relationship with Him even more than we want to accomplish that in our lives. Elijah salted the water at the altar for God and lifted his voice to proclaim a stop to barrenness and death in the land and to bring forth fruitfulness. Salt purifies from all impurities in the natural, just as we want to do in the spiritual.

The pure water of life flows from the throne of God and waters the trees of life with healing flowing through its leaves in every season (see Rev. 22:2). We water the garden where life grows. It is where people dwell in peace and communion with God. The battle was over the tree of the knowledge of good and evil. The knowledge and desire to know evil cuts off the fullness of life. It began the strife in relationships. God wants to restore that peaceable Kingdom and harmony in the land. The rest of the Bible is God's pursuit of humankind to restore them back to the Garden.

The law of Moses set forth specific regulations to prevent disease and provide a sanitary model of hygienic health practices. The Mosaic sanitary code provided for periods of Sabbath rest, dietary rules to reduce bacteria, sexual prohibitions against incest and other unnatural relations, cleanliness through washing the body and clothing, and sanitary procedures for armies to prevent the outbreak of epidemics of infectious diseases (see Deut. 23:12-13).

Prevention of psychosomatic illnesses is also assured through obedience to the Word of God. *"Pleasant words are as an honeycomb, sweet to the soul, and health to the bones"* (Prov. 16:24 KJV). Good health was intended to flow from an integrated wholeness of body, mind, and spirit. The psalmist spoke, *"Why art thou cast down, O my soul? and why art thou disquieted within me? hope thou in God: for I shall yet praise Him, who is the health of my countenance, and my God"* (Ps. 42:11 KJV). Forgiveness and cleansing from sin will bring health and healing (see Jer. 30:12-17; 33:6-8). The redemptive healing work of Jesus is the greatest healing force known to humankind. Guilt, anger, bitterness, envy, jealousy, and other negative emotions bring in sickness to the soul. Love is the one antidote to psychiatric illness that can save humanity from the many diseases produced from our evil nature. Therefore, the new commandment of Christ is foundational to physical and mental healing and health (see John 13:34).

God's Divine Healing Prescription

God first declared Himself the God who heals. He proclaimed this after He showed the Israelites—through plagues He deliberately put on the Egyptians—that He was the God they needed to heed. Then, He declared His healing to the people. *"If you diligently heed the voice of the Lord your God...I will put none of the diseases on you which I have brought on the Egyptians..."* (Exod. 15:26). When God declared this He longed for their obedience. He gave a new commandment that through honoring Him there would be blessings of life and productivity in all that they set their hand to do. The land would be healed and produce crops, the wombs of the women would be opened and life would come forth. Many blessings would cover the people as they honored God.

Obedience to God's Word and an attitude of mercy enhance health and healing. A healing and prospering blessing comes across a nation of people as they honor and obey Him. No disease is impossible for Him to cure. No limitations are listed. Testimonies of healing are listed throughout the Bible and recoded with detail by Luke, the doctor.

Jesus considered it normal for people to go to the doctor (see Matt. 9:12). He sent people back to the doctor to confirm their healings. In the parable of the Good Samaritan, oil and wine were poured on the wounds of the beaten traveler (see Luke 10:34). The woman with the issue of blood had spent much money on going to many doctors, and her condition went beyond the knowledge of the doctors of her day (see Luke 8:43). Paul chose Luke to be his traveling companion and developed an important model of an apostle and healing doctor traveling together to minister to the full healing needs of the people (see Col. 4:14).

God used additive actions to activate the faith of the sick person to bring their healing. For example, Naaman, the leper, had to step into the Jordan River to cleanse his leprosy (see 2 Kings 5:14). Jesus put a salve of his spit on the eyes of a blind man (see Mark 8:23). He made a salve of clay and spittle, too (see John 9:6). He also used the laying on of hands and the anointing of the sick with oil as symbols to impart the divine presence and power.

Divine Healing Utilizes Medical Remedies

Many healings in the Bible were accomplished by some visible means, while others were without means. Some were by a person's faith, and some came to a person with no faith. Different patterns emerge, but God deals individually with each situation.

We should not think we must choose between God and the doctor. The rejection of medical remedies revealed by God through the wisdom of doctors in favor of divine healing *is not a reasonable act of faith in God.* God may lead certain individuals to step out in trust and dependence on faith, but Scripture does not seem to indicate that this needs to be the general rule for healing by faith. Many Christians have received healings through surgery and regimes of medical wisdom. And we should pray for God's help in medical research to recognize healing ingredients God put in the earth. The leaves of the trees do have healing ingredients that can be medicinal. Many discoveries of modern medicine have been used for healing of diseases and stopping viruses from spreading.

Spiritual Roots of Sickness

Four causes of sickness are found in Scripture:

1. *Separation from God and others as the consequence of the curse from Adam and Eve's sin.* In this sense, all sickness stems from humanity's first sin. However, it does not follow that personal sickness is always due to our own personal sin. The fact that there is a tree with all manner of fruits for the healing of the nations does indicate that sickness is the result of original sin and is to be removed, even as the curse brought about by that sin will be removed (see Ezek. 47:12; Rev. 22:2; Rom. 8:18-23; Gen. 3:18-19). Negative emotions cause distresses from ill feelings in relationships. This separation causes a love hunger that brings stresses into people's lives, making them vulnerable to emotional and physical

sickness. Psycho-immunology shows the mind's role in vulnerability to sickness.

2. *Man's ignorance and carelessness.* This can be due to lack of sanitation and cleanliness in Christians that don't realize the contagious agents in the environment. As knowledge of medicine increases, many diseases decrease and life spans increase. Community education in third-world countries can help to alleviate these environmental risks.

3. *Individual sin.* Sickness can be directly involved with human sin, like sexually transmitted diseases from sexual relationships outside the marriage covenant. Chronic illness from addictive smoking or drinking is another consequence of sin. Jesus commanded a chronically ill man to be healed, saying, *"...Behold, thou art made whole: sin no more, lest a worse thing come unto thee"* (John 5:14 KJV).

4. *For development of character.* Just as a father trains and develops a child, so does Father God allow sickness and accidents for good purposes in our lives. Romans 8:28 says, *"All things work for the good of those who love the Lord."* Paul said his thorn in the flesh kept him humble. Job recognized his pride through his afflictions. Jesus not only healed but also forgave people of their sins. Jesus often healed people, saying, *"Your sins are forgiven,"* as with the paralytic man (see Luke 5:18-26). The fact that Paul healed others yet suffered with sickness himself shows that God feels it is good for some to have sickness because of what it is doing in their spirit. This also shows healing is dependent on God's will rather than just on our faith. Paul had faith, but it was not God's will. The prayer of faith is according to God's will.

The gospel of grace that Jesus carries provides a foundation for God to heal when and as he pleases. So even though principles are set in motion, he moves in mysterious ways to draw us to his ultimate goal, that we would only believe (see John 6:29).

God's Will in Healing

Jesus was moved by compassion to heal. There was a compelling in His Spirit to heal when He saw or heard of peoples' needs. When Mary came weeping about Lazarus' death, Jesus was deeply troubled in His Spirit and wept. Then the Jews commented on how much He loved Lazarus, but He asked her to take Him to the tomb and was deeply moved again as He said, *"Take away the stone,"* so He could call him back to life (John 11:39).

When a leper questioned Jesus as to whether it was His will to cleanse him of disease Jesus didn't hesitate. It was always His will to heal. He never turned people down who came to Him for a healing touch. He longs for people to come to Him as their Healer. That is His essence—to heal and restore. In His mission to undo the works of the devil, He made every effort to cast out demons and heal every disease. His ministry was to body, soul, and spirit. His goal was the restoration of the entire personality of the person. He had a heart to redeem people back to Himself. His miracles and healings showed the early Church His power and authority. But His disciples moved in the same spirit and showed that the Spirit made that power available to others. The healing that His disciples demonstrated showed the power and authority of Jesus. And it was a trademark that they were followers of Christ. Philip's miracles at Samaria and Paul's healing of the cripple at Lystra opened opportunities to tell of Jesus (see Acts 8:5-6; 14:8-10). Jesus, as in the case of the man born blind, healed some who initially had no faith (see John 9:1-38).

Healthcare Policy

Family Research Council Director Tony Perkins united with Lou Engle's The Call International Prayer movement, along with congressmen and senators, on the eve of the congressional battle for healthcare reform in December of 2009. This was an effort to reestablish God's reign as Healer over the healthcare proposal by the government. I participated in the meeting on Christmas Eve, praying for the merging of policy and prayer, and praying for God's people to take a stand for righteousness on the issue of life. The issue of life is the foundational issue in God's healthcare.

God created life, sustains life, and redeems life forevermore. He preserves life from the moment of conception, establishing Himself as the One that sets the days of our lives on earth from the first to last. He determines the day we come into the earth and the day we pass on to eternal life. Extend your hand to the needy just as the Lord extended His hand to you.

Nations call fasts to humble themselves before God and seek His healing in the land. But the true fast that touches God's heart is not just to cry out to God for help but to do the social justice He calls for. All God's people are called to extend their hand to minister God's care in tangible ways. We bring His care in pragmatic ways, and we bring His caring presence in abiding in Him.

The end of the Bible reveals Him calling us all to come to Him. The Spirit of God and *we,* His Bride, extend His call to come to Him (see Rev. 22:17).

Come to Him and get three things–

Rest, Revelation, and Restoration

Jesus said, *"Come to Me...I will give you rest"* (Matt. 11:28).

Rest

We quiet our hearts to hear His voice and know it well. We are the friend of God so He can share the deeper mysteries with us. We are coming to God for healing, hope, and peace, like a child going to his father to make it better. Dad takes her in his arms and calms her spirit, assuring her that it will be all right and Dad will always be there for her.

Going to God is like getting the peace to our bodies. We calm our bodies, and our biological systems can heal. God applies the healing balm of His loving kindness, His goodness, and His mercy in our situation. We realize He is watching over us and we are in His loving care. He is singing over us, building a new song in our lives. We find new things to rejoice in even during the struggles we experience. We find new praises as we see Him at work in our lives. He never leaves us or forsakes us in our sickness and trials. We can rest in that assurance and receive His blessings as we connect with Him. We come into His presence and receive His power to heal.

As we rest, the Lord arises. He arises to shine, to open the gates and unlock the doors with the keys He has given us. The Lord will arise in me and shine through me! As I rest in Him, He will make my paths straight and heal my sicknesses as I wait. He clears the way, freeing us from our bondages. He restores what was lost as I yield to His paths, and He leads the way.

Revelation

> *"Give attention to my words, incline your ear to my sayings...for they are life to those who find them, and health to all their flesh"* (Proverbs 4:20-22).

His word spoken is the healing agent as we receive it in our hearts. *"He sent his word and it healed them"* (Ps. 107:20). As we rest in His presence and hear his healing Scriptures, we realize the goodness of the Lord. And we experience its healing power in our lives. We enjoy His redemptive love and begin to connect with His plans and purposes. We get revelation of His love for us and our love for Him. Then He reveals to us His perspective on things. It helps us understand His holy purposes in our struggles. We are like Job who suffered sickness, loss, and death in his family, but his greatest struggle was to understand what God was doing and why. When he got revelation of who God is and how He works, Job calmed down about his own struggle and prayed for his friends. At that point, God healed and restored his health and prosperity.

This opens the way for destinies to be fulfilled. *Sickness steals life, but revelation restores life.* It restores meaning and purpose to what we are going through. We begin to understand the Scriptures. These present sufferings are nothing in comparison with the glory that is revealed in us. Truly, the glory is beginning to shine as our countenance is lifted and we see God at work in us. We relax in the revelation and open our hands to receive. We open our hands and our hearts for the gifts of the Spirit in the time of struggle. This is why we can praise Him in our problems. We see new life and meaning springing forth. We realize God's heart is to give us what our hearts desire, but we must come to Him to get the gift. He shows that He is here for us; we just have to go to Him and He will provide. His eye is upon us and His love is covering us. We understand the truths. Jesus loves me; *this I know! His loving word is the healing agent in our lives.*

Restoration

> *"I will heal them and reveal to them the abundance of peace and truth...it shall be to me a name of joy, and an honor before all the nations, who shall hear all the good I do to them"* (Jeremiah 33:6-9).

Restoring peace and unity comes first in our connectedness with God. Then relationships are restored, and last comes healing for our bodies and minds. Being in relationships brings our body, mind, and spirit back into peaceful balance.

The Spirit of God breathed into Adam and Eve to first bring life into them. That same breath of God breathes healing into our bodies and spirits. As we sit before Him in prayer, His Spirit breathes a new life that brings wholeness. It goes to the root of our emotional past and breathes His healing love into it. This assures us that His love covers past sin and shame.

Emotional wholeness flows out of this abiding in the presence of the Lord. He speaks wisdom that helps us keep His perspective on the things of life and the central concern on God's heart: "…*Guard your heart, for it is the wellspring of life*" (Prov. 4:23 NIV). A person's heart is the center of values and protection of the mind, emotions, and will. The mouth speaks out of that which fills the heart. Let it reflect a heart connected to the perspective of God. The outflow of the heart determines the way one speaks, relates, and behaves (see Matt. 12:34). And it becomes peace and joy overflowing as a living testimony to others.

Heart Connection for Healing

No matter the past, present, or future concerns, *the heart at peace with God heals.* The heart that realizes God's love, God's presence, God's care, and God's healing will bring a life flow of healing, purifying, oxygenated nourishment to breathe new life and wholeness.

Our team went to minister to a woman with end-stage cancer in the infusion clinic. She was very ill but had strong faith and a vision for her future testimony for God. Her faith kept her strong and vibrant though her body was weak. As we looked from the perspective of the nurses' station at all the people in their rooms with open doors, we saw the woman we prayed with was as sick as the others but had a glow and vibrancy about her that was unlike the others. Faith made the difference in her countenance and her perspective, though her body had the same degree of ravaging sickness.

Healing Hearts and Fulfilling Destinies

We are in a season of time when God wants to heal our hearts and draw them back to Him so that we may be strong for Him and fulfill the call He has on our lives. He has need of us in the turmoil today. He needs Kingdom-minded people establishing His Kingdom wherever we go. He needs us to get over our wounds and never, ever give up on the call He puts in our hearts. He is ready to send the resources needed for us to fulfill the dreams he put in our hearts, and He wants us to get over the emotional and physical wounds that bind us and hold us back from focusing on the call He has before us.

When patients realize their purpose and destiny in life, they are more motivated to fight the sickness, whether it be emotional or physical. Patients tend to rally and heal when they see a reason beyond themselves.

God is doing a global move to redeem hearts and souls back to Himself. He is building His Kingdom on earth. So He needs us to bring our sicknesses and weaknesses before Him to get healed and be restored to be part of His holy army.

Jesus experienced every emotion we do, but He kept everything in perfect balance. His holy personality example to us comes to fill our minds with vision for how to live. For physical balance, we are to care for our body like it is a temple of the Holy Spirit. For spiritual balance, we are to become conformed to the image of Christ. We are to take on the mind of Christ for mental balance. For emotional balance, we are to connect with the emotions of Christ. All four areas connect with each other. We cannot neglect even one to lead a balanced, healthy life.[1] We cannot allow toxic emotions; we must live to a higher standard.

Endnote

1. Dick Mohline and Jane Mohline, *Emotional Wholeness* (Shippensburg, PA: Destiny Image Publishers, 1997).

Chapter 3

Clinical Medicine's Original Design for Healing

Hippocrates is widely known as the founder and father of medicine and the originator of the Hippocratic Oath, used in medical schools today for physicians' ethical medical practice. Hippocrates was a Greek physician born in 460 B.C. Hippocrates held the belief that illness had a physical and rational explanation and rejected views of his time that illness was caused by disfavor with the gods. He was the first to reject supernatural forces in the cause of disease. He separated the discipline of medicine from religion, believing that sickness was not a punishment inflicted by the gods, but rather an impact of the environment, diet, and living habits.

Hippocrates' reaction to establish clinical medicine while dismissing the spiritual component of healing has led the medical profession to be missing a critical component of healing that should have been in their healing arsenal all along. People are dying prematurely because the spiritual component has been missing.

The Hippocratic Oath does not mention spiritual factors in illness. It sticks to ethical healthcare practices, and is all about honoring and respecting life. Hippocrates believed that the body should be treated as a physical whole that needed rest, good diet, fresh air, and cleanliness. He did note individual differences in severity of illness and that some people were better able to cope with disease than others. He also developed an intellectual Hippocratic school of medicine that revolutionized medicine in ancient Greece, establishing it as a discipline. His medicine included the behavioral arts that were kind, gentle, and sterile.

Leaves Bring Healing Ingredients

A medical mission to Zaire took me to a primitive culture that gives understanding to the ancient cultural beliefs to which Hippocrates might have been reacting. Africans believed that the gods healed or brought curses on your health dependent upon how they felt about you. The Africans couldn't see germs, so they thought germs were gods the Westerners feared. They did ritual practices like cutting the skin over the place where the pain was to let out the demons they thought were causing the sickness. When their witch doctors walked through the American hospital they thought surgery looked like the same thing. They thought you should open up the skin and take out the thing that is bad and hurting. They believed a spiritual intervention could remedy the illness and got results from their incantations. They would speak a curse over someone and put them in the white man's hospital and watch them die without the doctors being able to determine a cause. Life and death are in the power of the tongue (see Prov. 18:21).

Africans also were very responsive to Christian spiritual prayer for healing. They expected to see results in response to prayer as it was a most needed method of healing in their culture since their medical resources were limited and largely dependent on missionary doctors. Their expectation level was so high that they saw the result of a healing prayer in a powerful way.

An African elder of the Nyankunde, Zaire, church had a wife who had been incapacitated for ten years with a psychiatric disorder so severe that she laid in bed in a fetal position and was out of reality. Missionary doctors had tried many treatments including shock treatments and found no cure for her. Her husband asked me to pray for her healing. Her psychiatric sickness was well-known, as she was so disordered and the wife of a prominent leader. He and a nurse took me to pray for her. As we anointed her and prayed, I could feel her husband's love for her touching the heart of God. I felt the power of God flow like electricity through my arm and into her.

She abruptly sat up and recognized her husband for the first time in ten years. Suddenly clear minded, she thanked me and said she would come to my rehabilitation clinic as soon as she got cleaned up. News of her healing spread throughout the villages, and the next day hundreds of people had walked to our clinic to see me and wanted to know Jesus. I asked why this made such a profound difference to them, and they surprised me by saying, "We thought Jesus was for the next life when we go to Heaven, but now we know he has power in this life so now we want to know Him now." Just one healing changed the Nyankunde hospital procedure, and we called for all the African pastors to bring their Bibles right into the clinic and show people the Jesus they now flocked to find.

Another medical mission occurred in Iraq when our medical director, Dr. Doe, and I encountered a man with back problems. The Muslim man came to our medical clinic asking our American doctor if he thought the man should have cuts put on his back to release the demonic activity that he thought caused his back pain. Our American doctor said, "No, Jesus already took the lashings on His back for your healing. Now we can just pray to Him for your healing."

The Muslim man said, "OK, please pray to Him for my healing." After we prayed and anointed him, his back was healed and he was so moved at the healing that the next day he brought his whole family to the clinic for prayer.

As we anoint and lay hands to heal we find the power of God releasing healing through us as Jesus' healing touch is observed right in the medical setting even if the patient isn't a believer in Jesus.

So we pray and see what God does, and provide whatever medical services are needed. But God's specialty seems to be to show Himself faithful when medical treatment seems to not have the resources to heal.

Seeing is believing! Seeing God move and heal brings a convincing in people's hearts. The power of the witness raises expectation levels in the family and community to God's power to move. Literally, the kingdom of God is at hand.

The Hippocratic Oath

The Hippocratic Oath (Modern Version)[1] was updated by the Declaration of Geneva. The General Medical Council provides guidance in the form of duties of a doctor and good medical practice.[2]

> "I swear in the presence of the Almighty and before my family, my teachers, my peers, that according to my ability and judgment I will keep this Oath and Stipulation.

> "To reckon all who have taught me this art equally dear to me as my parents and in the same spirit and

dedication to impart a knowledge of the art of medicine to others. I will continue with diligence to keep abreast of advances in medicine. I will treat without exception all who seek my ministrations, so long as the treatment of others is not compromised thereby, and I will seek the counsel of particularly the skilled physician where indicted for the benefit of my patient.

"I will follow that method of treatment which according to my ability and judgment, I consider for the benefit of my patient and abstain from whatever is harmful or mischievous. I will neither prescribe nor administer a lethal dose of medicine to any patient even if asked nor counsel any such thing but perform the utmost respect for every human life from fertilization to natural death and reject abortion that deliberately takes a unique human life.

"With purity, holiness, and beneficence I will pass my life and practice my art. Except for the prudent correction of an imminent danger, I will neither treat any patient nor carry out any research on any human being without the valid informed consent of the subject or the appropriate legal protector thereof, understanding that research must have as its purpose the furtherance of the health of that individual. Into whatever patient setting I enter, I will go for the benefit of the sick and will abstain from every voluntary act of mischief or corruption and further from the seduction of any patient.

"Whatever in connection with my professional practice or not in connection with it I may see or hear in the lives of my patients which ought not be spoken abroad, I will not divulge, reckoning that all such should be kept secret.

"While I continue to keep this Oath inviolate may it be granted to me to enjoy life and the practice of the art and science of medicine with the blessing of the Almighty and respected by my peers and society, but should I trespass and violate this Oath, may the reverse be my lot."

The original Hippocratic Oath was one of the first statements of moral conduct to be used by physicians, assuming respect for all human life—even the unborn. It was known as a condemnation of abortion and infanticide.

Healthcare and the Church

Hospital patient treatment in institutions with specialized staff was begun by churches and charitable organizations as refuges for lepers, the poor, or pilgrims. The first Spanish hospital, founded by the Catholic Visigoth bishop Masona in A.D. 580 at Merida, was designed as an inn for travelers to the shrine at Merida, as well as a hospital for citizens and local farmers. The hospital's endowment consisted of farms to feed its patients and guests.[3] The first hospitals founded in the Americas were the Immaculate Conception Hospital and the Saint Lazarus Hospital in Mexico, opened in 1524 to care for the poor. In Europe, the medieval concept of Christian care evolved during the sixteenth and seventeenth centuries into a secular one. In the eighteenth century, the modern hospital began to appear, seeing only medical needs and staffed with physicians.

The adoption of Christianity as the state religion of the Roman Empire drove an expansion of the provision of care. The first Nicea in A.D. 325 urged the church to provide for the poor, sick, widows, and strangers. Monasteries provided lodgings for poor people and travelers. They also treated the sick and infirm with a separate section for lepers. The Good Samaritan story in the Bible tells of the use of an inn for an injured man.

Dr. Luke's Good Samaritan Healing Model

Jesus' story of the Good Samaritan shows a wounded man who was passed over by those who would have been expected to care for his emergency healing need (see Luke 10:25-37). First a priest, then a Levite passed him by. They were the two in that day who would be expected to bring healing care. The priest represented the pastoral leader, and the Levite represented the prayerful intercessor. But Jesus makes the point that a Samaritan journeying by a wounded man was moved with compassion. That could be any person going by. But this socially despised person brought help.

Social prejudice caused Jews and Samaritans to not be in fellowship with each other. Jesus broke down social division with compassion for the needy. Social groups and religions of the world may have their differences of theology. But when it comes to the sick and injured, the compassion of Jesus crosses all barriers and brings help. So He uses a healing lesson to bridge cultural and religious differences. Everyone can come to the healing well for Jesus to bind up their wounds. He shows mercy to heal. No matter the culture or religion, Jesus is the source of healing. He shows the Good Samaritan bandaging the wounds, pouring on healing oil and wine as anesthesia, and taking him into the inn to care for him. And he paid the innkeeper two denar to care for him. Jesus' love responds to all human need. He calls us to follow His model of care-giving and go and do likewise.

First Psychiatric Hospitals

The first hospitals in the Persian Empire included sections for the psychiatric cases, and the first psychiatric hospital was in Baghdad in 1705. In ancient cultures, religion and medicine were linked. The earliest medical facilities were Egyptian temples. Since then, in different religions, the church or temple took in the sick, and today one-fourth of people still go to religious-based medical facilities.

The Power of Prayer

Dr. David Larson, president of the National Institute for Healthcare Research, says research focusing on the power of prayer has nearly doubled in the past ten years. Now they are funding a prayer study through the Frontier Medicine Initiative. In a holistic medicine article, "The Proof that Prayer Works," many scientific studies were reported, including a National Institute for Healthcare Research panel to determine the merits of integrating conventional medicine with behavioral and relaxation therapies. They found that prayer was the key component.[4] Cardiologist Dr. Randolf Byrd studied 393 cardiac patients in the coronary care unit and noted that patients who were the object of intercessory prayer had dramatic results. They needed fewer drugs, had less need of ventilators, required fewer antibiotics, experienced less edema, and were less likely to die.[5]

Dr. Harold Koenig, M.D., and psychiatrist at Duke University, wrote the *Healing Power of Faith in Medical Care*.[6] Dr. Koenig observed that patients active with religion were happier and healthier than nonreligious patients. He also noted some religious patients experienced "miracles" in their health. His review indicated abundant scientific research about the role of faith healing in that was often overlooked. He documented 1,200 studies on the effects of religion and health. He noted religious people lived healthier lives. They tended not to smoke or drink and ate healthier foods. Heart patients were 14 times more likely to die in surgery if they did not participate in religion. Elderly people who didn't attend church had a double rate of strokes. And in Israel, religious people had a 40 percent lower death rate from cancer and cardiovascular disease.

He noted that religious people tend to become depressed less often and for a shorter duration. Dr. Dupont of Rockville found religion significant in addiction recovery as patients realized that God had a purpose in their lives. Dr. Koenig noted that 12-step overcomer programs were the difference between life and death with alcoholism patients. Hope and healing came to these self-absorbed people as they realized there was a God greater than themselves who could heal them and give them purpose in life.

Conventional medicine may not always meet the needs of patients, handling their illnesses in the emotional and spiritual realms. The healthcare team could take a spiritual inventory as part of their social history and determine if they want to pursue spiritual needs as part of the healthcare process. They do need to be matched with caregivers who have similar belief systems.

Dr. David Larson, M.D., M.S.P.H., is the spokesperson for the International Center for Integration of Health and Spirituality, and he has studied the impact of spirituality on health for 20 years. His review of the literature shows a positive link between spirituality and medicine. Dr. Koenig conducted a study with African-American women in early stages of breast cancer at Johns Hopkins University School of Medicine. He claimed religion provides patients with a worldview that gives them a more optimistic attitude that helps them cope better with illness. It helps provide purpose and meaning in the illness process. Other studies showed prayer positively affected them.

Healthcare today should be a health-based program rather than disease-based program. We should be finding ways to create an environment for health and healing. The Mayo Clinic offers alternative therapies and shows that prayer by families, for families, for patients, and by patients improves results in the healing process.

Medical science is discovering that emotional health can govern physical health. Stress has been found to increase the risk of cancer. Children raised in violent homes can have developmental delays.

WebMD Medical News reveals people who are prayed for fare better.[7] The power of prayer evidences that in medicine, as in all of life, prayer seems to work in mysterious ways. In vitro fertilization clinic studies had higher pregnancy rates when total strangers were praying for them.[8] And people with risky cardiovascular surgery have fewer complications. Dr. Rogerio Lobo of Columbia University School of Medicine, without knowing about the prayer, noted the women "prayed for" were pregnant twice as often as other women.[9] The second study appeared in the American Heart Journal. Dr. Glen Justice, M.D., reported research has been going on a lot longer than has been reflected in medical journals. He noted from the studies that you don't have to believe in it for prayer to have an effect.[10]

A recent study of cardiac patients conducted at St. Luke's Hospital in Kansas City, Missouri, concludes that intercessory prayer may indeed make a difference. "Prayer may be an effective adjunct to standard medical care," says cardiac researcher William Harris, Ph.D., who headed the St. Luke's study.[11]

Science has given many advances in healing, but God demonstrates His sovereignty over medicine when patients no longer respond to medical treatment. That point is that even unbelieving patients desperately turn to prayer; some find peace and comfort in coping with chronic illness or death, and some find healing solutions beyond what medicine could provide. God did create our bodies to heal themselves, and He can heal them beyond science.

Can God heal when science has reached its limit? These patients show the most convincing results when doctors have no more solutions and patients heal beyond the medical prognosis. Physicians often don't have an explanation of the healing and frequently say, "You were lucky," or "You had a miracle." The Book of Acts documented supernatural healing, and God's Word says He is the same today as He was before (see Heb. 13:8). It says we can do greater things than Jesus did, so biblical truth confirms healing stories that medical staff refer to as "God stories" (see John 14:12)! Ukrainian doctor Yoon-Seok Chae, a surgeon from South Korea and president of the World Christian Network, reported that the same miracles, signs, and wonders performed 2,000 years ago are still taking place even today.[12]

Behavioral Science Restoration

In my experience with the Behavioral Science Faculty at the Hershey Medical Center, in a research study of the role of faith in cardiac patients, interviews revealed that many patients during cardiac arrest had experiences of leaving their bodies and seeing a light or, in some cases, having conversations with Jesus. Often, they didn't tell others, thinking people wouldn't believe it was authentic. But having a person who believed these experiences were authentic freed them to tell of their experiences. Those who had similar experiences had such an inner peace that they said they no longer feared death, and they had a new sense of purpose on earth, realizing they had a second chance at life to do something for God.

We also noted in the rehabilitative department that people with the same diagnosis will have varying responses to their disabilities and will accomplish a variety of achievement levels, depending on their emotional and spiritual response to it. Faith tended to give people more of a sense of purpose to look beyond their physical limitations and strive for a better lifestyle and a mission to live to accomplish. One's response to disease tends to minimize or maximize the level of handicap depending on the value a person thinks they get from it and other purposes they see for their life.

Miracles and Medicine Together

In the 1970s, Oral Roberts pioneered the integration of faith healing and medicine after what he felt was a vision and word from God telling him to build the City of Faith, a 60-floor skyscraper hospital. He said God told him to:

> Build the City of Faith to capture the imagination of the entire world about merging My healing streams of prayer and medicine. I did not want it localized in Tulsa, but the time has come that I want this concept of merging My healing streams to be known to all people and to go into future generations.

God told him, "You and your partners have merged medicine and healing for the entire world, for the Church, and for all generations." God told him then to close it after eight years, saying, "You have accomplished it in the same way my Son accomplished on the Cross the culmination of a three-year ministry." On the Cross Jesus declared, "It is finished," and He had accomplished His mission to impact the world forever.[13]

When Roberts first began, God told him, "Son, you cannot put the vision I have given you into a place where My full healing power is not freely accepted. It must not be in a place defeated by lack of faith in My miraculous power. You must build a new and different medical center for Me. Healing streams of prayer and medicine must merge through what I will have you build."

Other quotes from Roberts that hit the media were:

- "Expect a miracle."
- "Something good is going to happen to you today."
- "God wants you well. God wants you prosperous. God wants you a whole person."
- "God came to take off you what the devil put on you, to take out of you what the devil put in you, to put back on you what

the devil took off you, and to put back in you what the devil took out."

- "I respect doctors, and one reason is that they have grasped this eternal truth and are against sickness and for health. Consciously or unconsciously, they have a pretty good theology of healing. Sometimes I wish we Christians had such a good theology of healing. Then we might be less inclined to argue about whether it's God's will to heal or not."

- "In the midst of the turmoil, the fear, the anxiety that's in our nation and in our world, as I was walking and meditating, I heard the voice of God. I've heard that voice many times; it's familiar to me, and there's no way that I can fail to understand it's His voice because I am familiar with it."[14]

Other faith healers have impacted medicine, like Kathryn Kuhlman in Pittsburgh. She held healing services in a church near Mercy Hospital and had a packed room of patients in hospital beds and wheelchairs brought to the church to get a healing touch from God. Kathryn maintained her healing center in the church, always wanting to point people not to the healing but to the Healer. Her focus was on worshiping God, and in that atmosphere would come the healings and miraculous activities of God.

Today, teachings of Lance Wallnau have brought a new season of faith among the worldwide church that God first established. The influential mountains of society are impacting government, education, the church, the family, and the media, and God wants to restore them to Kingdom purposes in this season.

God first established the divine law out of which our constitution and legislative system were birthed. He first established rabbinical teaching out of which sprang schools of education. He first established the Good News of the Gospel and the first Bible out of which came the printed word.

Now that pioneers of healing in society have had their season of demonstrating how healing and medicine can come together, we can take healing prayer back into the hospitals and enhance the healing process. Healthcare will no longer only heal physical symptoms, but it will bring healthy lifestyles and cause people to learn to live healthy lives spiritually, emotionally, and physically. It is time to return to Jehovah Rapha who taught the principles of healthy living.

Live Healthy Lifestyles

All the health streams converge with the wisdom to live with healthy nutrition, healthy relationships, healthy thinking, and a healthy relationship with God! We especially want to guard the treasure within us by guarding ourselves from destructive thinking, harmful foods, and harmful relationships. The phrase, "Don't worry, be happy," reminds us to get over our focus on our sufferings and lift our focus to godly perspectives and the world will be a better place.

Live beyond your disease and your fight for healing. Live for your purpose in life. Battle the physical and emotional cancers in your life that grow like destructive cancer cells and destroy your destiny.

Endnotes

1. Ludwig Edelstein, *The Hippocratic Oath: Text, Translation and Interpretation* (Baltimore, MD: Johns Hopkins Press, 1943), 56.

2. General Medical Council, "Good Medical Practice: The Duties of a Doctor Registered with the General Medical Council," Parkingspa.com, http://www.gmcuk.org (accessed March 26, 2010).

3. "Hospital," Wikipedia, The Free Encyclopedia, History, http://en.wikipedia.org/wiki/Hospital (accessed March 26, 2010).

4. Holistic-online.com, "The Proof that Prayer Works," Prayer and Faith Healing, http://1stholistic.com/Prayer/hol_prayer_proof.htm (accessed March 26, 2010).

5. Larry Dossey, "Healthy thinking: Praying," June 2003; http://www.odemagazine.com/doc/5/healthy_thinking_praying/ (accessed May 15, 2010).

6. Harold G. Koenig, *The Healing Power of Faith: Science Explores Medicine's Last Frontier* (London, England: Simon and Schuster, 2002).

7. Jeanie Lerche Davis, "The Power of Prayer in Medicine," WebMD Medical News, November 6, 2001, http://www.webmd.com/news/20011106/power-of-prayer-in-medicine?page=3 (accessed May 15, 2010).

8. Ibid.

9. Ibid.

10. Ibid.

11. Dr. William Harris, archives of Internal Medicine, October 25, 1999.

12. Dan Wooding, "World Christian Doctors 'vote for miracles' during Unique Conference in Kiev," Breaking Christian News, http://www.breakingchristiannews.com/articles/display_art.html?ID=7281 (accessed March 26, 2010).

13. Oral Roberts, *Quotes from Oral Roberts Christian Prayer Center* (Tulsa, OK: Oral Roberts University, 2009).

14. Ibid.

Chapter 4

Balancing Cultural Beliefs and Healing

Where people place their faith and belief tends to bring re-sults as they pursue that avenue of healing. A Nigerian nurse explained it well as I asked her whether she and her African colleagues believed in faith healing. Her answer surprised me. She said, "We have no choice but to believe in healing. We don't have the medicines and medical expertise you have in America. If we didn't have healing from God, we wouldn't have it at all. We have to rely on God's healing." Then she asked, "You mean your people don't believe in healing?"

When I explained the theological debate we have among dif-ferent denominational circles she couldn't believe it was even a question to discuss. Her response stirred me to see the power of where we put our faith and where we receive our healing. She had a pure faith that we have lost as we have gotten more reliant on medical science. She sees divine healings in her country that we long for in ours. She is a nurse and trains people in healthy lifestyles, like cleanliness and good nutrition. And she will use medicine when it is sent to her. But her reliance and trust is in the only place she can trust to see healing.

Her culture trusts in God's power like America trusts in medical science. This sheds light on words Jesus often spoke as He responded with divine healing and said, *"The Kingdom of Heaven is at hand"* (Matt. 4:17). He also said, *"Daughter…your faith has made you well"* (Luke 8:48). Faith in medicine causes us to call the doctor, and faith in Jesus causes us to call upon God and see His compassionate response. We can reach out to touch the heart of God and His compassion will flow freely for healing today.

First Nations' Healing

The American Indian First Nations' view of health is, "Living your life in balance according to the natural laws of the Creator."[1] They believe the human mind, spirit, and emotions must be in balance to be healthy and that disease is a manifestation of a person's imbalance among these aspects. That the body maintains itself in balance and has a natural ability to self-heal and recuperate. They want to bring a person's body, mind, and spirit into a deeper knowing of the Great Spirit to facilitate the body's own recuperative powers. Annette Cyr says their healers treat the whole person, identifying the underlying causes of sickness and treating them, and they move to remove all obstacles to facilitate the inherent healing process. This is in contrast to treating and eliminating symptoms of disease. Their aim is to bring alternative therapies to complement clinical treatment strategies, believing that culture will enhance the science of healing.

Deliverance in Cultures

African and Middle Eastern cultures have more of a sense of spiritual warfare and are more aware of the power of demonic activity than Americans tend to be. They see the power of blessings and curses and want God's power over evil. Jesus declared His disciples would have power over evil so believers need not fear. Their words carry the power of God to bring the truth and light to overcome the power of darkness. But direct confrontation in that battle, as in any other battle, brings casualties. A power encounter can bring needless casualties. A truth encounter is easier for those inexperienced in spiritual battle. Jesus spoke Scripture to the devil in the desert, and the power of the Word and Jesus' belief in the Word caused the devil to flee, realizing his tactics to undermine faith were to no avail.

Spiritual battles are in the mind. It was the first strategy the devil used against the first woman. He tried to undermine her faith in God's word to her to not eat of the tree of the knowledge of good and evil. If she had heeded the voice of the Lord rather than the undermining voice of satan, she would have stayed in close fellowship with God. But listening to the undermining voice and acting on what it said separated her from intimacy with God.

In the same manner, we need to ignore the undermining words we hear that negate faith in the Word of the Lord. We need to close the door on those claws that try to bring us down. The voice of the Lord edifies and strengthens us to fulfill His purposes, but the voice of satan causes doubt and shame, lust and bitterness—all manner of destructive thoughts that separate us from the love of God, love of others, and love of ourselves. As soon as we let those deceptive and destructive thoughts come in to our minds they destroy faith and relationships and open the door to sin and sickness. Anger sets in, depression sets in, and we spiral down to our biological systems, becoming depressed as well and losing immunity to sickness.

Power encounters or truth encounters can end the battle swiftly. We can take authority over soul sickness and body sickness by speaking the name of Jesus who already did the work of over-coming death of every form. We can plead the blood of Jesus for our protection. There may be unconfessed sins that need to be brought to light and repented of and renounced to clear any stronghold the enemy may have for repeated attacks. Then we turn our heart and minds to worship of the Living God and give thanks for the great things He has done.

David did that in many psalms. He first expressed his complaint and discouragement before God and then remembered the good things the Lord has done, and his spirit was lifted and the depression gone. Keeping focus on the words of the Lord and His goodness gives no room for the enemy to discourage our souls, and our blessings and destinies are birthed as we worship the King of kings. Make no room for the enemy in your thoughts or behaviors, and sickness will be defeated and destinies fulfilled.

Jesus the International Healer

Out of our chapel prayer ministry at Penn State Hershey Medical Center came the opportunity to go to Iraq, to the UN-declared no-fly zone, which would become the place of healing and refuge for people to feel safe and not need to leave the country. A doctor coming from another hospital to see the medical center prayer service ministry asked if we would take a behavioral science team to northern Iraq to train Muslim doctors to do family and community medicine. We would do behavioral health issues training for emotional and spiritual health effects on physical healing and well-being. Thirty doctors came for training sponsored by the Duhok Department of Health. They shared their concern that, though their medical training was good, people weren't healing due to the stresses of living in a war-torn nation where it was common to lose family members from bombings and land mines.

Death was so common to them that they said they stopped having emotions 15 years ago to be able to cope with the trauma.

During our training of the Kurdish doctors, we told of the Amish schoolhouse shooting tragedy in our region that gave us a taste of the trauma and pain they experienced. A surprising healing effect happened that sent a message in the media coverage around the world. The Amish bishop responsible for the families who had daughters shot went to the family of the killer and offered forgiveness and compassion to help the killer's family heal. The forgiveness helped alleviate the pain and sent the message out to the world that forgiveness heals.

As we shared the story of the Amish forgiveness with the Muslim doctors, they tried to find a word to translate this healing principle. They had trouble finding a word for forgiveness because it was a new concept to them. As they began to understand the meaning for forgiveness and the healing effect it has on the perpetrator and the victim, they reacted by saying that this was a brilliant concept and that they wanted to be "Amish-ized" if that was what brought healing in hearts and between people.

The head of the Department of Health wrote on the board in front of the doctors learning this new concept Gandhi's quote: "An eye for an eye makes the whole world blind." At that moment, they realized holding hatred in your heart perpetuates sickness, and forgiveness was the remedy to release the healing. Recognizing this principle that forgiveness heals, the Department of Health leader stood proxy as a government official asking for forgiveness of the other doctors for what the former Saddam Hussein regime had done to the Kurdish people. He asked for forgiveness for the Enfal operations that had gone on in the region and said he wanted to be a government official that would bring healing and not heartache. Tears came down the doctors' cheeks as they heard these healing words. A new, lighthearted attitude grew in the doctors during our training that caused other hospital workers to come by and wonder at the joyful spirit in our classes. The new spirit of joy was spreading, and others wanted some, too. In preparation for our next trip, the Department of Health set up the Zanest Family Medicine Center to do community healthcare training.

My travels to the Middle East cultures where they believe in the Qur'an and Torah bring surprising findings. Our first trips to Iraq, as guests of the health department to train their physicians in healing, yielded surprising conversations. We discussed the bodily effects of emotional and spiritual responses as we talked about the limitations of medicine in bringing healing where war and trauma have brought so much stress that people tend not to heal even when medical attention is given. Muslim doctors readily recognized that the Qur'an talks more about Jesus than Mohammed. They believe enough in the legitimacy of healing by Jesus that patients flocked to receive Jesus' prayer to bring healing to their bodies. They did receive healing and such a strong sense of Jesus' love for them that they brought family members who weren't sick because they wanted the healing prayers for them as well.

The same happened in Israel. When people were extended the opportunity for healing prayer, they lined up for hours to get a healing touch of God. The love and peace they feel when touched by prayer makes them long for that personal touch from God. Reports come back consistently of not only healings but answers to prayers for jobs and family relationship healings. Various unfulfilled needs are answered by faith reaching out for a touch of God.

Paul wrote, *"Now is the accepted time; behold, now is the day of salvation"* (2 Cor. 6:2). "Salvation" refers to healing, being set free from bondages, and prosperity. Jesus, who brought these healings 2,000 years ago, still does these healings to those who reach out to Him for it. Father God sent Him to earth to demonstrate to us

His divine love. He demonstrates through healing His personal care for us so that we would respond to His love.

> *Then great multitudes came to Him, having with them the lame, blind, mute, maimed, and many others; and they laid them down at Jesus' feet, and He healed them. So the multitude marveled when they saw the mute speaking, the maimed made whole, the lame walking, and the blind seeing; and they glorified the God of Israel* (Matthew 15:30-31).

When we are healed God gets the glory and people are drawn to return to God.

In Isaiah 61 and Luke 4, Jesus' purpose is stated—the anointing of the Lord was upon Him to bring good news to man, to preach the Gospel to the poor, to heal the brokenhearted, to proclaim liberty to the captives, and to bring recovery of sight to the blind. The joy of the Lord was in His healing of all sicknesses and sufferings that held us in bondage. The Lord has jubilee for us in His Kingdom coming.

His healings confirm His Word and come in power by the speaking of His Word! *"He sent His word and healed them, and delivered them from their destructions"* (Ps. 107:20). This destroys the work of satan, who came as the thief to try to steal the abundant life Jesus came to bring (1 John 3:8).

Psalms declares: *"Bless the Lord, O my soul; and all that is within me, bless His holy name! Bless the Lord, O my soul, and forget not all His benefits: who forgives **all** your iniquities, who heals all your diseases"* (Ps. 103:1-3). This is the foundation for believing prayer that all healing is available through the salvation of the Lord.

Consequently, Jesus' anointed life purpose and His sacrifice for our sins laid a covenantal foundation for our redemption from sickness and sin. Isaiah 53 shows the tremendous suffering Jesus took upon himself for our benefit. It was the will of God to bruise Him; He has put Him to grief and made Him sick (see Isa. 53:10). He was bruised and chastised to bring us peace, well-being, healing, and wholeness. He is our intercessor, pouring out His life unto death (see Isa. 53:12).

Matthew 8:16-17 captures the heart of the Father working through Jesus by restoring to health all who were sick. He bore our diseases on His back, and they were carried away from our concern on His back. We can yield them to Him, and He will heal and remove them from among our midst.

Endnote

1. Annette Cyr, "First Nations," Traditional Healing, Culture as Healing, http://traditionalhealing.suite101.com/article.cfm/first_nations_traditional_healing (accessed March 27, 2010).

Chapter 5

Who Carries Authority to Heal?

Believers are people who have put their faith in Christ. They carry the power to heal because they carry the Spirit of the God who heals. Believing prayers in the chapel have demonstrated time and again that God continues to bring divine interventions in the healing process that demonstrate results beyond medical explanation. For example, we have seen tumors on medical scans disappear by the time the doctor goes to remove it in surgery.

According to Jesus, *"And these signs will follow those who believe: In My name they will cast out demons...they will lay hands on the sick, and they will recover"* (Mark 16:17-18). The disciples went out to preach, and even after the Lord ascended into Heaven, by the Spirit of God the Lord was working with them and confirming the word through the accompanying signs that followed.

Greater works than these you will do. There is a reality of the power of God flowing in the lives of believers. The Lord says,

"Most assuredly, I say to you, he who believes in Me, the works that I do he will do also; and greater works than these he will do, because I go to My Father" (John 14:12). The Lord is the source of all healing. Modern medicine has wisdom from God for healing, but doctors know they have their limitations. Many conditions, such as cancer and heart disease, elude a final cure.

Miraculous healings have been reported throughout church history. Medicine and healing arts are gifts from God and are used to minimize suffering. But ultimate healing is created by God and goes beyond what medicine can do. When doctors say there is nothing more medicine can do, God can do more. He is the Creator, Sustainer, and Healer. He is the ultimate Healer and source of all healing. Whether it comes through modern medicine or divine healing, God is the supreme healer. He clearly stated, *"I am the Lord who heals you"* (Exod. 15:26). And He continues to demonstrate the truth of His word.

The prophet Isaiah spoke in Isaiah 61 and Jesus confirmed his word in Luke 4 that the spirit of the Lord was upon Jesus to preach good news and to heal. The Book of Acts documents that the apostles could do even greater works by the same anointing and spirit. The Lord said that those who believe can do greater works. We need to believe the Lord and lay hands on the sick and watch them recover. The twentieth century brought a new breed of healing evangelists like Kathryn Kuhlman, Aimee Semple McPherson, and Oral Roberts. This is our time to step out and take God at His word. We are called to arise and shine in this later season of time. Let the glory of the Lord flow out of you with the Spirit's anointing. The heart of the Gospel is the good news of Jesus and what He did for you. Faith comes by hearing the Word of the Lord, and then there is healing in response to it. There is power in the gospel as it impacts a life. Healing flows in response.

Simple Acts of Faith Release Miracles

Working in a rehabilitation clinic, I noted one day that a stroke victim paralyzed on one side didn't come for therapy. So I went to his room to see what had happened. He was blue and unconscious and had just suffered a massive heart attack. I took his hand and spoke: "Charlie, it's Abby. I am praying for your healing." As I spoke the prayer I noticed a power surge of an electrical-type sensation in my arm going to his limp arm. Then I noticed his blue face started turning pink and returning to normal color.

Doctors rushed him to Massachusetts General Hospital, thinking he had a massive heart attack on top of his stroke. But upon arrival, he had been healed to perfect health. He had no symptoms or signs of a stroke or heart attack as found by admitting physicians. They sent him back to the rehabilitation hospital wondering what was wrong with the diagnoses by the rehabilitation doctors. Those doctors were surprised and embarrassed by the seemingly wrong diagnoses. Charlie told them and came to me to say, "Your prayer healed me and saved my life." His doctors came to me to discuss the impact of prayer on him as well. We carry Kingdom authority, and it impacts others in a powerful way as we are going about our daily activities. Next I got a call from the chaplain of Massachusetts General Hospital asking me to do rounds with him and pray for patients in that hospital. We visited patients together and faith was built through the neurological unit as patients with multiple sclerosis and other neurological disorders got healed.

Some of our healing prayer team took a mission to Mali to pray for healing for orphan children. They prayed for blind eyes to be healed and visibly saw the milky appearance turn to deep brown eyes as they laid hands on them and prayed. Healings happen when we lay hands on a person and pray. Just as Jesus traveled from city to city to take His Gospel to them and God demonstrated the power of His Kingdom by doing healings as he went, we carry that same spirit of authority if we just believe and pray for people as we go.

The Prayer of Faith Makes the Sick Well

The prayer of faith with the laying on of hands imparts God's healing power to people. Fervent prayer among believers who boost one another's spirits impacts others. The healing communities who pray fervent, believing prayers are contagious and strengthen the weak and suffering. There is a healing balm that strengthens the sick. Surrendering to the Lord is the key to releasing the anointing of the Lord.

> *Is anyone among you suffering? Let him pray.... Pray for one another, that you may be healed* (James 5:13,16).

People tend to share their family concerns, having a sense that the sickness may have brought a halt in their lives and they must get back on the right track. The teams should listen with the grace of God. No matter how shocking it can be, they are confessing it to get God's help. His response would be like it was to the prodigal son—loving and forgiving. Jesus often told a healed person not to sin anymore.

"The effective, fervent prayer of a righteous man avails much" (James 5:16). Fervent, earnest, heartfelt believing prayers of people walking in right relationship with God carry power and authority to bring healing as they are compelled by and access the heart of God. Often Scripture says Jesus was moved with compassion to heal. *We* should also be moved by the compassion of God to heal.

These words are strengthening and edifying. They speak life and truth from God's Word.

Receiving healing means opening your heart and spirit to receive without letting fears and concerns block your ability to receive God's love and healing power.

Anointing of the Spirit of God involves healing balm from ingredients from anointed leaves of the garden. He himself took our infirmities. He is our burden-bearer—the one who takes the accusations, bitterness, and spoken words against us upon His back. His stripes are the propitiation of our iniquities. Through His sacrificial love for us we have access to healing if we hand over our guilt and shame, our anger and anxieties, getting the burden off our bodies and freeing ourselves to be restored to health.

Spoken prayers of righteous people who live in godliness can change the cellular structure of our bodies to restore healthy cells that have been damaged. Through the hands of many apostles, many were healed (see Acts 5:1-12).

Chapter 6

Healing Prayer Model in a Medical Center Chapel

The prayer ministry that happens in the medical center can serve as a model for establishing a prayer ministry in any business, school, or government facility that wants a prayer center where people can connect and receive prayer for their personal and healing needs. Other healthcare businesses have become interested in similar prayer ministries in health-related industries such as insurance companies and drug stores, for example. Imagine the health benefits of healing prayer at work, reducing the need for sick days, doctor bills, and insurance benefits. Also think of healing prayer being offered to students in school. Milton S. Hershey school students wanted to have a place of comfort for their special emotional needs. Recognized staff of the school adopted the model for healing prayer and offered it in a safe environment for their students. This healing prayer altar is a model that can be replicated in many cities and healing institutions. In fact, think of it being offered in mental healthcare for women in crisis or in addictions centers. Most people seem to have healing prayer needs for themselves or family members.

Ministering to Unbelievers in Crisis

This is not the same as believers normally ministering in the church where there is already a culture of belief in God's help in healing. Jesus didn't stay in one place. He went to the temple, but He took His disciples from city to city to minister to the people where they were. We are like Jesus and His disciples going to the temple to be personally equipped, then taking the healing ministry out to the cities in secular settings where most people have never experienced prayer ministry and many do not attend any religious institution. Some do have faith in other gods or other styles of belief, but few know the personal healing touch of God for the needs in their lives. Out in the community, this ministry is a welcome surprise to people who tend to be deeply moved by the personal care and healing results.

Jesus didn't keep his healings in the churches; in fact, He walked from city to city and healed the sick as He went. He carried the Kingdom of God within Himself, and when it brought a healing touch to their lives people were moved to greater faith as they saw the convincing love of God. It was personal ministry Jesus used to demonstrate God's love and the power of the Kingdom of God, drawing the hearts of the people as He looked into their eyes and spoke life-giving words. The power of God was in His words and His hands, and people flocked to follow Him, to draw from Him some of His healing, redeeming love.

After Jesus was resurrected, Paul continued to carry Jesus Christ's spirit and message as he went into Athens and noted that they were worshiping many gods. Paul's spirit was disturbed as he saw the different gods they served in their attempt to connect with the God they did not know. But he was honoring in how he addressed them as he said, to paraphrase, "I see that you are faithful people. And I see your sign to the unknown God. I come to tell you of the God you do not know" (see Acts 17:16-20). Like Jesus, he did not come to condemn them but to offer them a gracious God who wants them to know His true identity. Healing is a way God brings His personal love and compassion to those who need Him.

Honoring the House

Paul's honoring the people of a city is a model of love and compassion which we follow as we enter the secular facility. We honor the house we enter and bring peace to it as Jesus instructed His disciples to do. We begin showing the compassion of Christ and bringing His edifying, uplifting, healing words of grace as we bring the Gospel in their time of need. They see for themselves that God is near, and they feel compelled in the spiritual atmosphere to share what they know they need to get in order in their own lives. So we become good news bearers to them. We do not confront people about their lifestyles or wrong faith choices. Instead, we show them the benefits of allowing the true *I am*, the Lord who heals, come and minister to them. Without the pressure of evangelistic conversion messages, people feel drawn to the God that cares for them. If they are drawn first, then they ask how they can get closer to the true God who hears and answers their prayers. And they often spontaneously confess what they know is blocking their faith in their lives.

Ministering to Families

Families often come together when a family member is in crisis, though they may not normally be in fellowship with each other. Suddenly, in crisis or grief they find themselves coping together and trying to make critical decisions as a family when other problems are looming in their relationships. The crisis will become a time of bonding or of distancing, depending on how they choose to react in this time. Believing family members come to the well and sometimes bring unbelieving family members to get help in time of need. Prayer ministers get revelation about the hearts of family members and how they can support each other in this time of need. Often, when prayer ministers show caring to the unbeliever, it softens their hearts to God.

Prayer ministers also give vision to believing families about how they can bring support to the family. One week, a mother and daughter came concerned about the father's health, and prayer ministers noticed the daughter's strength of faith. They encouraged the daughter to support her mother in the medical decisions, and a deeper courage came in their bond as they faced decisions together.

Balanced Treatment

The prayer ministry offers healing prayer support to enhance the medical process, not to negate it or work at cross purposes with it. We offer healing prayer as a support to strengthen the family in the medical process. We never tell people not to cooperate with medical treatment. If people believe they have had a supernatural healing, we encourage them to have further medical testing to verify the healing and let doctors adjust treatment programs as they see the evidence of the healing.

They hear the call over the hospital intercom and see the sign outside the chapel beckon them in: *"Come, all who are weary and heavy laden, and I will give you rest."* Patients, staff, and visiting families in hospitals all have one thing in common. The stress of crises brings a need for a place to find a respite of peace and rest. They need a refuge to turn to for a sense of being able to come before God and call upon His help. Most people seem to come in to rest their weary bodies in the chapel and find a bit of solace as they cry out to God, hoping He will hear in that place. They share their burdens and find caring, listening ears from the prayer team that will join their prayers for their stated needs. They are so relieved to find support as they come before God on behalf of their health concerns. And they find as they enter the room they feel they are entering a holy place where they sense the peace of God enveloping them.

It is as though God is saying to their spirit, "My light will shine, My love will live, and My spirit will dwell in those who choose to enter My presence." The invitation goes out over the hospital announcements that meditative healing prayer is available in the chapel. Medical staff delight to find support in knowing they can come for their own needs or the needs of their patients. They know they can meet others who will appeal to God on behalf of their expertise in dealing with the health issues they need to care for in the medical center.

Call for Wisdom

Medical staff can find the wisdom for healing in the life-giving psalms and proverbs of God's Word. As they focus on the truths of God's Word in the peaceful atmosphere, their concerns dissipate and their spirits are strengthened with wisdom and hope in the living God who cares for them. Focusing on the medical concerns in the context of the spiritual report of the Lord through His words of truth helps restore life-giving faith and hope as they experience the presence of the Lord's loving care over their lives. It is like dwelling in the protective shadow of the almighty God (see Ps. 91:1). It is like coming to a place of refuge in the midst of sickness and tragedy in the crisis environment.

Faith comes by hearing the words of God that align weakened spirits with the bolstering truths that revive faith. A renewed spirit of peace brings tears to their eyes as they experience His strengthening words ministering in the valleys of life. His words bring healing streams bubbling up in their hearts. They literally gain a new perspective, knowing it is in God's care. Often people weep and find a release of the stress they have been carrying as they begin to share about the burdens their family has been experiencing. Having prayer ministers listen and give comforting words and prayers brings a peace and healing to their hearts that is desperately needed and a welcome surprise in the face of a medical trauma center.

The wisdom of God planted where the wisdom of medicine flourishes brings the best security to know that human wisdom is boosted by God's wisdom and healing power. Patients can trust they are in the best hands for care, but they trust in God for the ultimate outcome, knowing that God is with them as they go through this process.

Pray Together, Flow Together

The healing team joins together an hour before the service to stir their hearts and ministry gifts to flow together in the chapel setting. Hearts are prepared for team ministry as they worship and share their inspirations for the day. Themes generally emerge as they join their hearts in prayer. The pastoral team leader watches over the team and those coming in for ministry to guard the flow of the anointing of God for healing and to discern ministry needs as people come in.

The pastoral leader is like an orchestra conductor as he or she watches over the worship and how that coordinates with what God is ministering in the chapel. An atmosphere of worship is maintained throughout, and the worship seems to speak personal messages to hearts as the healing needs are brought into the room. A caring hospitality person is posted at the door to the chapel to welcome people and ask about their prayer need. Then guests are ushered into the room according to what they came to receive. They may want to first sit in the room and observe the worship and prayer ministry until they feel comfortable sharing their need. Generally, it only takes a few minutes until they ask for prayer. If they are the only one asking for prayer and want the full team to pray we share their need to everyone in the chapel. Then a few who sense a prayer for them gather around to lay hands on them and pray. The team always asks if it is OK to lay hands and to anoint them. And we are sensitive to not overwhelm them with too many "pray-ers" surrounding them.

A Healing Touch

Everyone that reaches out to God for healing help will find it. Everyone that comes to the chapel will find needs ministered to. Just like the woman who slipped through the crowd to get a touch of Jesus' robe and receive the healing virtue, so it will be for all who enter in to the altar ministry. Jesus says to the degree that you seek Him you will find Him. Ask, seek, and knock and the door will be opened to you (see Matt. 7:7). Faith in reaching out to God will bring healing fruit in every life.

Jesus invites us to draw near: *"For everyone who asks receives, and he who seeks finds, and to him who knocks it will be opened"* (Matt. 7:8). Go in to Him and ask. A door is opened in Heaven. *"Come up here,"* says the Lord (see Rev. 4:1). We go to Him, and He draws us in nearer to Him. We get our healing touch of His presence and it touches our soul.

There is hidden power in healing prayer. Step in and receive the healing that is yours. All who carry the compassion of God may enter in. Draw near and enjoy the depths of His healing love from His heart of compassion.

A Dose of God's Medicine

Coming to the chapel is like a dose of peace, comfort, and renewed hope and strength from the Father God. God's Word provides promises of hope to hold. Some cancer patients come to the chapel before their chemotherapy infusions and receive a spiritual strength infusion as they hear the soothing words of truth. God's sayings are like life to us and health to our flesh (see Prov. 4:20-23). Attached are words of health and healing for our bodies.

Obtaining the wisdom of God is to be our principal goal in life. In addition to providing life and healing, it will bring protection over our life. *"Hear, my son, and receive my sayings, and the years of your life will be many"* (Prov. 4:10).

Be discerning in balancing medical wisdom with faith in God's word over your life and health. We need to have a balanced focus to cooperate with medical wisdom but believe in what the Great Physician can do as He is watching over us. He is faithful to speak to us, strengthen us, renew us, and restore health to our spirits, souls, and bodies.

Remember, the enemy of our souls is the father of lies and will try to deceive us and take away our health and strength. When Jesus has already accomplished our healing in the spirit realm, let us continue to agree with God's Word on the matter. Meditate on and confess His Scriptures so they become part of your heart that He is redeeming for Himself. Let the redeemed of the Lord *say so!*

Give thanks to the Lord for He is good; His mercy and loving kindness endure forever (see 1 Chron. 16:34). We remember the blessing of the one leper out of ten healed who returned to the Lord to give thanks. We know the power of people returning to the chapel to give thanks for healings received and strength given in times of grief. We thank God for those who return and give thanks. It is a boost to the prayer team, the person giving thanks, and others who hear and gain hope for their situation.

> *Bless the Lord, O my soul, and forget not all his benefits* (Psalms 103:2).

I remember a Muslim woman who came to the Muslim prayer corner to pray during our healing prayer time. But she couldn't concentrate on her prayers because she heard people coming into the chapel to praise God for their healings. She came out of her prayer posture in her prayer room to watch what we were praying.

Healing Benefits of Praise

There is a healing assurance that comes when we have thankful hearts. The psalmist cries, *"All that is within me,"*—my entire being praises (see Ps. 103:1). There is an inward stirring that brings remembrance of blessings, healings, redemption, and soul satisfaction that relaxes our body to better receive healing benefits. The praises benefit national blessings as well. The Lord executes righteousness and judgment prompted by prayers on behalf of the people. God is not only righteous and just in Himself, but He engages in these acts for the oppressed in the land.

The psalmist also praises God for the benefit of *forgiving love*—so great is His fatherly mercy that restores us in our frailty (see Ps. 103:11-14). The *eternal love and grace* of Father God are there for the taking. The extension of His love is conditioned by human response to the covenant and commands of God in proper reverence and awe (see Ps. 103:15-18). This is the crux of the matter to receive healing. The next verses call for *universal praise*. If the people over all the earth recognize and receive the love and healing of God, then the sun of righteousness could arise with healing in its wings (see Ps. 103:19-22).

Pray and Praise to Overcome Sickness

Though there may be many needs for deliverance and healing, the focus in the chapel is on worship and praise of the healing works the Lord does. In the atmosphere of praise and love of God, people's faith is bolstered. Their sense of the Lord's love and acceptance of them is built, and they start letting down their defenses as the soothing atmosphere makes them feel loved by Father God.

One man covered with tattoos and piercings came to the chapel and was overwhelmed by the love he received in contrast to the judgment he often received when people looked at his tattooed and pierced appearance. He always felt judged by the Lord's people. But in this atmosphere of Christ's love, he opened the door to issues in his heart that needed healing and found deep healing to his injured heart. This is the approach we take. We share the healing love of Jesus, and when the people feel loved it pours a healing balm into the hurts in their heart.

James 5 Prayer Prescription

It is interesting to note the order listed for healing prayer and anointing in James 5. This is the first combination of medicine and prayer used in biblical days. Anointing in Bible times was actually a mixture of oils thought to have healing benefits that they put over the wounded area as though applying a healing balm as they prayed. So they were applying healing balm as a medicinal remedy combined with prayer. Today we anoint with an olive oil or other anointing oil that we believe is symbolic of God's anointing as we pray. The scriptural prescription listed from James 5:13-18 is as follows.

1. Anyone who is sick comes to the leaders for prayer.
2. The prayer of faith will save the sick, and the Lord will raise him up.

3. If he has sins he will be forgiven.
4. Confess your trespasses to one another, so that you may be healed.
5. The effective, fervent prayer of a righteous man avails much.

Healing is a mystery and a gift from God that comes in various means and methods. Chapel ministry prayer does not require confession as a prerequisite to the healing prayer and anointing unless the healing fruit seems to be hindered and the patient is open to sharing. When people begin to experience the healing effect they naturally feel compelled to share their transgressions on a deeper level when God's healing love already makes them feel safe to share. Then they share from a heart of gratitude for God's love for them, and they open up to share their confessions. A deeper, more sincere healing response comes out of confession and gratitude for God's healing touch. This is better than if they are first asked to confess their sins to qualify for healing prayer. In the loving atmosphere, God may give words of knowledge through the prayer ministers, but they must be in harmony with the loving spirit ministering to them. And their visions and words must flow with what God is doing at that time.

Often, the revelation that comes flows so freely that the patient receives a deep, life-changing healing of emotional bondages, which then frees their body to heal of rippling physical effects. A spirit of affliction over them can be loosed and they are free to heal. People often experience a setting free from bondages that bind them, and the spirit of Christ helps them overcome sickness and suffering. The prayer team can watch for signs and symptoms of underlying causes of sickness as they interact with the patients.

When our hearts are filled with fear and anxiety, hormones are released to the alpha and beta receptors and all parts of the body are affected. Muscles, blood vessels, gastrointestinal tracts, vascular beds, insulin, and bronchi are all being affected and impacted by stress.[1] When the heart is at peace, or rest, then the rest of the systems can heal and go back into homeostasis. Fear and stress then are a root problem causing many diseases. The heart at peace with God and our situations in life put things back in order.

The antidote to fear is communion with God. *"For God has not given us a spirit of fear, but of power and of love and of a sound mind"* (2 Tim. 1:7). Power comes from the Holy Spirit, love is from the Father's love, and a sound mind is from the Word of God.

Healing often begins when we make peace with God. The washing of the Word of God cleanses and sanctifies us, keeping our hearts purified before God. This regular going before God keeps our hearts and then our bodies in alignment with God. The fruit becomes evident in our health, our relationships, and our success in what we put our hand to do.

Prayer Altars of Faith

Establishing our spiritual, emotional, and physical health before God helps us to carry the presence of God in our hearts to impact others around us. It is like Peter walking through the towns and his shadow touching and healing people (see Acts 5:15). Our lives carry the essence of God and impact others in a powerful way.

In biblical history, altars were a place of sacrifice. For the patriarchs of the faith they became a place to worship and thank God. Noah offered a burnt offering of each kind of animal or bird that had been preserved in the ark. Abraham built several altars where God did significant things, like the most famous faith story where He spared his son Isaac. Moses received a word from the Lord that the tabernacle should have two altars. He called for a brazen altar for burnt offerings in the courtyard and an altar of incense in the holy place. The golden altar, or altar of incense, was placed inside the temple before the curtain of the Holy of Holies. It was where God's majesty was honored by means of burning incense. They were intended to be a place of worship of the true God. The golden altar is symbolic of intercessory prayer or a symbol of judgment (see Rev. 8:3-5). These altars of faith become a place where people can have a sense of coming before God, like going into the Holy of Holies.

As we look into windows of how God ministers to people's souls, we see He spoke through what seemed to be humble, natural means, but He was doing divine ministry to people's hearts. He put his kingly Son in a humble manger. He spoke to Moses in a common burning bush, except Moses noted it never was consumed in the fire. We live by unlikely signs that we could dismiss if we don't watch to see what God is doing. We have a responsibility to handle accurately the quiet workings of the Lord. They are messages of the King, and we must not miss them. We should receive them as words from God.

In Lord Alfred Tennyson's "The Coming of Arthur," his warriors cried in the *Idylls of the King*, "Be Thou King, and we will work Thy works who love Thee."[2] Around our banquet table in our ministry inn, God is about His business, calling warriors in his Kingdom for kingly purposes. They hear words spoken to them beyond what humans would speak. Some words are spoken by people in the natural and some are sensed in prayer as God's still, small voice. What we hear causes us to understand what God wants to produce in our lives. Our hearts sing, "Be Thou King, and we will work Thy works who love Thee." As we look around the room to each other we sense a temporary likeness of the Lord in each other, standing around God's table as though knights in service to the King of kings. He puts it all together. Intermingling the natural and the spiritual brings a reverent atmosphere of the holiness of God.

Destinies Called Forth

Healing happens at the altar, and it is the reason people come to God. Their needs draw them there. But healing from sickness is not God's end goal. In fact, it is the beginning goal. Jesus would often say when He demonstrated God's healing power that the Kingdom of God was at hand. He wanted to increase faith in God through healings and deliverances. But God conceived each one of us with distinct destinies for our lives, and once we are strengthened in faith and sickness is overcome we are prepared to have strength of faith and grateful hearts to fulfill God's purposes. Have you heard the expression, "Without vision, the people perish"? Without vision for their destiny, people get caught up in healing as their end goal. They think in terms of their sickness and suffering and how to cope with that or how to overcome it. But God wants them to get their eyes off their sickness and suffering and put it on His holy purposes. When they can focus on God's purposes they often suddenly realize their bodies are recovering.

Too often we can't get our minds off our pains and sufferings. We break down our own immunities when our focus is our pain. Just like David's depression healing when he focused on the Lord's goodness, sickness will lose its power over us when we focus on the destiny of God over our lives. When Job stopped questioning God and battling his sufferings and turned to praying for his friends, he then was released to have victory over his sufferings (see Job 42:10).

Just as God had a purpose for us before we were born, so did our parents have something in their hearts as they named us before they knew us (see Ps. 139:13-16). Parents have an inspiration or a desire for their children's lives as they identify a name for them. This practice was well-known as biblical parents named their children to speak of the meaning of each child's life. It still is highly regarded in some cultures, such as Middle Eastern names which carry destiny of purpose in people's lives.

We call forth the meaning of people's names and lives in the chapel even if they are children dying of cancer. We pray their names and the meanings of their names and the destinies that their lives carry. We ask God to not let their lives be cut short or their destinies unfulfilled but to let them have life and life abundantly, fulfilling every purpose in the heart of God for their life. Even if lives are cut short, the suffering of parents is relieved as they find some kind of purpose in their children's lives.

People generally have a good capacity to handle suffering when they find some meaning in the midst of the suffering. Just like Job cried out to God as to *why* he was suffering, we often have the same cry. We need an understanding. There isn't always an explanation except that God is good and He knows what He is doing. This is the answer God gave Job in the midst of his suffering. But Job began to heal as he understood God and prayed for purpose beyond himself. Then his life took its turn for the victory and redemption of things restored that the enemy of his soul had stolen for a season.

Revelations at the Wellspring

Healings happen at the wellspring and so do revelations about healing and how God moves. A mother brought her daughter in for prayer before tests; the doctors definitely thought she would require surgery. The team prayed, believing that no surgery would be required, but still encouraging her to go for the testing. The next week a message came through the hospital chaplain's secretary saying the mother wanted to thank us for the prayers because the doctors were shocked that the test came back saying no surgery was needed. The mother was so thankful for the prayer. And the secretary was amazed at the call about how the prayer really worked. Through a prayer for one medical test, the patient, her family, and her friends were impacted. And it was documented on a medical test that got doctors to see the medical result of prayer. The rippling effect went to the pastoral care secretary who got the call of thanksgiving for answered prayer, and she too was amazed at answered prayer.

As Jesus often spoke when He healed, the Kingdom of God is at hand. The Kingdom of God has a far-reaching effect to build faith in many through His healing demonstration of His power. When Jesus spoke that the anointing of the Lord was upon Him to preach good news and to heal and set free, He carried an anointing that we carry as His followers. That same healing anointing demonstrates His power to all who see and hear of the testimony of each life changed by God's healing touch.

Long-Range Prayer

Those prayed for in other states and hospitals demonstrate that the person being healed doesn't even have to be prayed over or know that prayers are going up for them. The impact of prayers can be far-reaching and unlimited. In fact, I emailed a Muslim man in Iraq to say I would pray for him for healing, and he received a healing through a vision in which I appeared to him with Jesus at my side and told him he would be healed and everything would be OK. The next day he was healed and discharged from the hospital, knowing that God was his Healer. There is no limit to how far-reaching the impact of the prayers can go.

Often as we pray as a team at the well, a spirit of prophecy rises up among the team and people get words of knowledge about the person and their family as we pray. Though we are only meeting them for the first time in the chapel, words start to flow and God gives revelation about deep issues in their hearts that need answers. He seems to speak a healing balm to them that satisfies their inner longings or questionings. In an instant, healing help is spoken from the heart of God for them beyond what human understanding would know to give.

Sometimes, pictures come that we don't understand. But if we speak them to the patient they weep with understanding because it heals something deep within. This is the deep river of life, flowing from the depths of God's heart and speaking to the depths of their heart. They suddenly realize the deep assurance that God was there all along. He was there when they had a heart's cry to Him and they thought He didn't hear. But He confirms that He was there, and it seems to heal something deep in an instant. The healing goes beyond what human wisdom could counsel, because only God knows the deep issues of their heart that need His healing touch.

A Typical Day in the Chapel

The prayer team arrives an hour before the noon prayer service and begins the prayer and worship. Soon, a mom comes in with her daughter Jen, who we have been praying for for several months. Jen had a massive bleed in her head for several months and was not expected to survive. Prayer was lifted for her life. She miraculously came out of the coma and her body bore massive stroke-like symptoms. Coming into the chapel atmosphere, her mother felt like she was to ask Jen to stand up and walk across the chapel room, walking for the first time since her head bleed nine months before. In faith, Jen stood up, keeping her eyes on her mother, who was coaching her to step forward while the team prayed with her. Jen took a step and then another and another. She did walk across the room, surrounded by the prayer team but walking on her own. Jen cried and her mother and father rejoiced.

We prayed God's healing love would strengthen Jen's body, mind, and spirit.

Then a mother of an infant came for prayer for her baby in surgery. She was so blessed by the prayer that she went to tell her unbelieving husband to come into the chapel for prayer. As soon as he stepped into the chapel he sensed the presence of God and felt compelled that he immediately wanted to receive Jesus as his Savior. We did pray with him to receive Jesus as his Savior, and we gave him his first Bible. He was so appreciative that he lingered in God's atmosphere.

Next, a Muslim man from Egypt came for his Muslim prayers, but he was an hour early so he sat in our prayer time. Soon, he told us he had cancer in his stomach and had had six out of eight chemo treatments. He let us pray for his stomach and was very blessed. Because his English was limited, we called an Egyptian doctor friend who invited him to an Arabic church service. The man was blessed by our prayers and watched our contemporary worship dancer dance in white like an angel in the room. He was so blessed by the caring prayers that next week he showed up for more prayer.

A grandmother of an orphan in the Milton Hershey School for Orphans walked in the room and was amazed at the ministry circles forming over different needs as patients and families came into the chapel. She went back to her church and wanted to teach others about the deeper life of faith she was learning. Only a few came at a time. But for each one it was a life-changing step of faith for healing. It is as though God orchestrates the timing of people coming into the room so that each one gets the prayers and personal care that they need.

Another man prayed his first prayer of salvation. Another man of another religion found healing in the Jesus prayer. A young staffer sat and prayed and watched as he found the reviving faith he needed to grow in his faith. He took his lunch break in our chapel prayers, as he enjoyed the reviving faith he experienced there. He told coworkers and his wife about the believing prayers that he experienced in the chapel.

Another woman came with a referral from her church to pray for a sick person. She led others in prayer. I told the stories to the chaplain's secretary and she was thrilled as she heard the stories, knowing God was moving every week in the chapel ministry. She said people would ask her about the service after seeing it advertised. God touched life after life as we told the stories of His wonder-working personal care for His beloved people.

Laying on of Hands

The healing team carries the heart and hands of Christ's anointing. The team is made up of caregivers compelled by compassion for the health crises families are experiencing. They draw from their own life experiences. Truly, as God strengthened them in their time of need, they want to strengthen others with that comfort they received from God. The team's prayers carry a spiritual Kingdom authority from having battled and overcome sickness and death in their own lives.

In the struggle, there is a strength that we receive that brings a greater authority as we personally battle and overcome things in our own lives. If you study the lives of powerful healing evangelists, you will find they learned to battle for healing through sickness and suffering in their own lives, and they gained a victory that bears great fruit in ministry. Healing ministry that began with Jesus continues to be exercised by His disciples today. We can experience breakthrough as we battle and overcome sickness in our own lives through healing prayer.

Just as Jesus demonstrated the victory for resurrection life in His own life, we carry the same resurrection life spirit in our lives as His healing ministers. The same authority that was on Jesus when He arose from the dead is upon the Christian prayer minister. Just as Jesus said, the anointing of God was upon Him to heal the sick and set the captives free, that same Spirit is available to us. We just need to activate our faith to be powerful and effectual.

Stoking the altar in the chapel with prayer every week for five years has established an anointed place of God's presence that remains in the chapel. Scripture says God inhabits the praise of His people (see Ps. 22:3 KJV). Where we come together to worship God even in a marketplace setting, we establish an altar to the Lord in that place, and creative miracles can happen in that atmosphere. After five years praying in the chapel, people notice a tangible presence of God as soon as they enter the chapel. They notice a burden lifted from their concerns and a relief that it is in God's hands. They feel a peace that relaxes their concerns like when anesthesia calms your body and concerns are gone.

> *Then they cried out to the Lord in their trouble, and He saved them out of their distresses. He sent His word and healed them, and delivered them from their destructions* (Psalms 107:19-20).

Three fathers came to the chapel for prayer one day not knowing each other. They arrived shortly after each other and ended up in the chapel at the same time to pray for their infant daughters. One was there to rejoice over his newborn daughter that day. The second father came to pray for his premature daughter who needed surgery. The third father was visiting his new daughter who he wouldn't see much because he wasn't married to the mother. That estranged father was moved as he heard the other fathers rejoicing over their daughters and praying for their new lives. He allowed us to pray for his role as a father and was deeply moved by the prayers. Coming to the chapel and receiving that personal touch made him want to go to church and get back to God. The prayers about his fatherhood stirred the desire in him to be a father to his daughter. His heart opened in the loving atmosphere and he was able to receive a father's love he wasn't sure he had.

Another young father had cried out in the chapel for his infant daughter with a broken skull. He was at a defining moment as to what would happen to her life and his. The anointed presence of God stirred a heart of godly sorrow and repentance in him. Some lives are rescued and saved as God tenderly draws them at His wellspring of life.

Barriers to Healing

People's inability to yield to the Spirit's healing has much to do with a lack of ability to believe that God could minister to them with divine healing. Barriers begin with unbelief, especially that God would care enough about them to work in their lives.

People tend not to see results when they refuse to open their hearts to believe. Immediately, they are putting up a wall to be unable to receive healing if they won't believe. Also, if they don't want to hear the Word of God and what it says about healing, they won't know what He can do for them. This is a trend, but God is not limited even by unbelief. Some people say they don't believe, and God still heals them despite their unbelief.

The biggest barrier to healing is unforgiveness. It locks hearts from being able to heal as they hold onto grudges toward others, toward themselves, or even toward God if they are angry about the sickness they believe He caused. Generally, they have been unjustly treated and have a sense of justice that won't let them release the offender into God's hands. To forgive is to release the grudge that holds you in bondage and hand it over to God to deal with them on His terms. When we let go of the grudge we free ourselves from its bondage, and we free God to do His work of healing in our life and deal with justice in the life of our offender.

People who hold on to secret sin often have health effects due to the built-up internal pressure they hold within. Once they confess it and change their addictive or ungodly behavior to right behavior before God and others, the healing will be released. Addictive behavior and ongoing sin operates as an idol in our lives that prevents us from benefiting from communion with the true God.

Lack of persistence in prayer to bring the healing result can cause us to fall short of the healing we are seeking. If the healing doesn't come in one prayer, we are called to contend for the healing until we receive it. Like the woman who kept persisting until the judge finally gave it to her, we need to persist until God grants our request (see Luke 18:1-8).

Repeated patterns of ungodly behavior perpetuate sickness in our lives. For example, repeated addictive behavior brings natural health consequences, such as smoking brings lung cancer. Liver disease is a direct result of unhealthy alcohol consumption. Sexual addictive behaviors transmit dangerous diseases as well.

Negative words spoken against us can weaken our bodies until we recognize it and don't allow it to affect us. This is why we need the spiritual armor in Ephesians to be in place, so any design of the enemy is deflected (see Eph. 6:10-20). No weapon formed against us can prosper if we know the truth, believe the truth, and behave the truth. Then our spiritual guard protects us.

Healing Cure—Repent, Renounce, Release

Repent of anything that binds you. Often bitterness or fear or deception render us prisoners to the offense and hinder our bodies and emotions from being able to heal. Intentionally acknowledging issues of anger at another person—or even feelings toward God or yourself—and repenting of unforgiveness will cause an immediate release of multiple health issues that have been perpetuated by internal stresses.

Renounce means to determine and commit to change your ways, saying, "I will no longer be involved in hurtful activity to myself or others. Nor will I let these behaviors continue to harm my health and relationships."

Release means to intentionally decide to let go of the attitude or behavior that binds you and prayerfully hand it over to God. Just as Jesus told the disciples to forgive seventy times seven, even the same offense by the same person (see Matt. 18:22). We must prayerfully put the concerns on Jesus' shoulders. He already settled them on the Cross and declared, *"It is finished"* (John 19:30).

The Kingdom of God is at Hand

Jesus often healed people and then told them that the Kingdom of God was at hand. He wanted them to recognize through the healings that Kingdom power for wholeness is present in this life. People may argue that they don't believe that kind of healing is for today. But Jesus is the same yesterday, today, and forever, and when they experience Jesus' healing touch they will quickly be impressed at what God is doing today.

The first healing that I experienced while my own personal theology said that healing wasn't for today was an arthritic woman who had one crippled leg five inches shorter than the other and wore a built-up shoe and walked with a cane. A healing prayer minister took her ankles in his hands, and as he prayed, I saw her shorter leg extend five inches so she could no longer wear the built-up shoe. The woman who walked in with a cane and built-up shoe jumped up and down and ran up the stairs in her stocking feet because she couldn't use her built-up shoe any longer. My theology changed right there as I saw God's healing touch change her life.

In the Bible, when the woman came to Jesus because her family was mourning over her daughter who had died, Jesus said, *"Do not be afraid; only believe"* (Mark 5:36). Then He took her by the hand and said, *"Little girl, I say to you, arise"* (Mark 5:41). Then her spirit returned to her and she arose. This happened to a teenage girl who had been burned to death. Her family was weeping and praying for her while she was having an experience of her spirit going to Jesus and Him welcoming her to Heaven. He asked her, "Do you want to stay here or go back?"

She said, "Forgive me for not serving You before. Let me go back and tell others about You." Then her spirit returned to her body and her body healed to the point of no visible burn scarring except for a scar on her head. Faith arose and her spirit returned. Let faith arise.

The Father's Love Heals and Redeems

The success of the Hershey ministry is in the Father God's redeeming love. It is the Father's love that built the town and His love that built homes for the orphans. The Father heard the cries of the orphans in those homes for 100 years and declared, "I will be back for my orphans who have cried out in their beds and I have heard them." God orchestrated a team of house parents to help in our healing prayer ministry.

Malachi 4 speaks of the fathers' love revival coming where the fathers' hearts are turned to the children and the children's hearts are turned to the fathers (see Mal. 4:6). Healing is arising, restoring families and the family of God. Divisions and accusations will be plummeted as divine love is restored. *"...You will receive power when the Holy Spirit has come upon you; and you shall be My witnesses"* (Acts 1:8 NASB). God gives a delegated authority to the healing team. Jesus' anointing is upon us. Believers can minister in the power of God at work in them.

> *The Spirit of the Lord is upon Me, because He has anointed Me to preach the gospel to the poor; He has sent Me to heal the brokenhearted, to proclaim liberty to the captives and recovery of sight to the blind, to set at liberty those who are oppressed* (Luke 4:18).

A Mother's Nurturing Healing Love

Jen had been having headaches since October of 2008, but the doctors said they were migraines. On March 14, we found out Jen had massive bleeding in her head and was to be airlifted to Johns Hopkins. They were getting the flight team ready when it was announced to Jen's family that she was going to surgery since they needed to relieve the pressure in her brain. Later, the family found out she would not have made it had she gone in the helicopter because of cabin pressure. God closed that door to save her. Later that night, the doctors told the family to say their goodbyes because she would not make it. They showed the family an MRI where her head was shifted from the brainstem.

Her mother said to the others, "I know what I see, but God is greater." And she headed to the chapel and told anyone who would like to come that she would be in the chapel. It became filled with Jen's family, friends, and coworkers. Immediately, she was put on prayer lists all over. Her mother got calls from churches and people she never met saying they were praying for Jen.

Her mom went down into the chapel on a Friday and was sitting in the back row praying when a member of our prayer group asked if they could pray with her. She said nothing, and the prayer minister realized and said, "You are Jennifer's mom, and we have been praying for her."

After that, she spent all her time in the chapel, and each week the prayer team would pray with her for Jen. She was in an induced coma and was in Penn State Hershey Medical Center from March through June. Then she went to rehab as inpatient until the end of September, and now she is doing outpatient therapy.

The doctors are amazed that she is here and by the progress she has made thus far. She went from a wheelchair to a cane. She visited the prayer group since Jen wanted to thank everyone and meet them. That day we prayed again, and Jen got up and walked without the cane.

God is not done with her, and we agree and believe for total restoration. The mother thanked us, saying that it was through our faithfulness and others, and God wanted us to be part of this *miracle!* Jen is truly a miracle and a testimony unto Him. No damage was done to her face and she speaks well; she has been a testimony to others who are in therapy with her. She is an inspiration to all of them from where she was to where she is now.

Her mother went with her to a doctor's appointment recently. It was a rehab doctor who was amazed and said he never saw anyone have that severe type of stroke that had come along so quickly. "Her prognosis is very good," he said, "and her attitude is great."

Her family sent the message:

> We as a family want to say thank you for your con-
> tinued prayers and support. Keep on doing what God
> has called you to do, it certainly is for a reason. We
> *praise* and thank *God* for His faithfulness and for what
> He has done for Jen. He will do the same for others.
> You cannot accept the bad reports; you must keep your
> eyes on the *Great Physician*, who has complete control.
> He works through doctors at times, but everything is
> in *His* hands. God bless each and every one who has
> prayed and stood for Jen. We will remember you all in
> our prayers. I pray that this gives hope to those who
> feel hopeless.

An eight-year-old boy was in the news when a rare bacteria
started eating his arms and legs. It was killing his limbs, turning
them black beginning peripherally at his hands and feet. Doctors had him in an induced coma while they tried treatments to
stop the blood poisoning in his body. Concerted prayer was collected when doctors were determining they needed to amputate
his limbs to stop the disease from killing him.

One day they were ready to remove his hands and feet and
our team went to pray over him before the surgery. We prayed
for a minimal loss of limbs, and for the blood poisoning to
stop its progression up his limbs. When finally he returned
from surgery, they had surprisingly been able to save part of
his hand and index finger. His mother was excited that he had
one finger left to lift his arm and finger to point to God for
saving his life. Her faith and the faith of many supporting the
family in prayer caused the young boy to have a great attitude
and still be active after recovery, playing with his friends from
his wheelchair.

Steward the Healing

The healing team needs to be open healing vessels of the Lord. They need to regularly guard the treasure of the healing anointing that is within them and by following these three keys:

1. God's healing vessels begin by making sure they have an unhindered flow of the Spirit. Repent of anything that blocks your own spirit. Make sure you are able to minister the compassion of Christ and have no strained relationships or personal emotional issues that hinder the love of God.
2. All glory goes to God. Make sure all glory goes to God and refrain from drawing attention to yourself.
3. Pay attention to the needs in others' lives and don't minister out of your own needs.

Medical center announcements can be made over the public announcement system, through the Internet, on posters, or by personal invitation. A regular weekly service should be advertised so people know when they can come for the prayer ministry. There is a standing invitation that people know all are welcome. Patients, staff, and family members—all are welcome.

"Come to Me, all you who labor and are heavy laden, and I will give you rest" (Matt. 11:28). This is the invitation to patients, families, and medical staff who all have in common the stresses and strains of a healthcare environment.

Healing prayer in the hospital chapel is a setting that provides the sick and distressed a place to come into as a tower of refuge from life's distresses. It provides a womb of healing within the hospital or medical center complex. It is a setting that can be filled with quiet meditative worship, dance, musicians, and healing prayer ministers. Candles are lit and chairs are set for comfort as they sit around the well.

The Meditative Worship

Quiet, meditative worship through CDs or instrumentalists invites people to bask in a soothing atmosphere to revive their spirits and pray for their concerns before God. Worship prepares the atmosphere for the Spirit of God to minister to the people. And it prepares the hearts of the people to minister spiritual healing. It also prepares the hearts of the sick to receive the healing impartation.

Worship blesses God and brings His healing presence as we thank Him. In our praises, our spirits are lifted and His presence becomes tangible. Faith comes alive as people experience the peaceful presence of God. And they can express their healing needs before Him and find answers to their fervent prayers.

Physicians in medical settings tend to be more open to prayer as a help to the healing process when it helps families cope with the stresses of illness, especially when medical care reaches the point where there are no more treatment options. However, physicians view it as a barrier when it impedes medical recommendations. Generally, physicians recognize that patients with faith and faith resources surrounding them tend to do better in the healing process. However, they don't want religious beliefs to trump medical care, and they get frustrated when faith healers interfere with medical decisions.

The presence of God releases God's activity all around and increases the experience of healings and miracles. Peace in the Spirit plays such a critical role in healing, peace, and reconciliation. It does not bring retribution, but peace in relationships. People's faith is stirred and their hopes are lifted. They find comfort that God hears and cares for them to strengthen their weary bodies and minds.

The Anointing

Compassion is what compelled Jesus and releases His tender mercy for people entering the chapel ministry. This compassion moved His heart to raise Lazarus, to heal sick children, and to feed the multitudes. Compassion comforts, heals, and opens hearts to receive. Paul went into Athens and saw they worshiped gods but didn't know the living God, and he didn't rebuke them but said he came to show them the unknown God. Neither do we rebuke people or cast out demons. Rather, we show the love of God for them and their concerns. In the compassionate atmosphere, people tend to be moved to tears and share their struggles. They are surprised to find prayer ministers in the hospital chapel, and they are refreshed by the idea that God loves them enough to meet them at their point of need and offer prayer and emotional support. People in crisis are vulnerable to ministry and share their deepest concerns in the presence of God.

Psalms 133:1-3 talks of the anointing being poured over Aaron's head and down his robe to cover him with the glorious anointing of the Lord, poured out like the dew of Hermon to command the blessing of life forevermore. We operate in the unity of pastoral people uniting in prayer to increase God's healing flow.

Keys to Releasing the Healing Anointing

Here are eight keys to releasing the healing anointing and waiting for God's anointing to come:

1. Jesus' *compelling love*. He was moved with the Father's compassion.
2. A *spirit of unity* releases anointing to flow like Jesus compelled people to be released in pairs.
3. *Encouraging words*. Begin with listening prayers to sense what the Spirit of God might want to do for them. Open

eyes and ears to listen for messages or watch for pictures the Lord might show you as you pray for them. Our team gets pictures and senses about them and shares them. With discerning words of knowledge, this can be a great inspiration to the person being prayed for. It provides a deep connection and message of what the Lord is doing in their family member. Sense what the Spirit wants to do in the prayers. Discern workings of the Spirit. Be sensitive to the warmth of the Spirit moving in you and in the person being prayed for.

4. *Ask permission* to lay on hands or anoint the person. Make sure they are comfortable with the prayers being prayed and the method you are ministering.

5. *Lay on hands to release the healing anointing.* God's love flows through us as we intercede on their behalf. Extend the believer's touch.

6. *Anoint with oil* as a seal of the Spirit in the prayers.

7. *Pray God's Word* and He will do what He has spoken.

8. *Use the name of Jesus.* His name lifted up draws all people to Him.

> *May the God of peace Himself* [God himself bringing peace] *sanctify you completely* [that your inner man is renewed]; *and may your whole spirit, soul, and body be preserved blameless at the coming of our Lord Jesus Christ* (1 Thessalonians 5:23).

Ministry is to bring an indwelling holiness that brings the gift of grace for new life. As Ezekiel said, God will give a new heart and spirit (see Ezek. 36:26). Grace first comes to the soul, then progresses to the body.

The Healing Word

The power of God's Word spoken carries the power of life and death. Our words can edify and strengthen a person or drain life from them. Life and death are in the power of the tongue (see Prov. 18:21). When a person gets a diagnosis that there is nothing more that medicine can do, he is discouraged and hope of life is drained from him. If he believes the word and loses hope for life, he stops fighting and tries to cope with the news.

God created, sustained, and heals life by His creative word. He first spoke, *"Let there be light,"* and there was light (Gen. 1:3). He spoke about making man in His image, and He breathed His breath into them to be filled with life from His Spirit (see Gen. 1:26). The prophetic word of a prophet can bring healing. In the chapel healing atmosphere, when a prayer minister gets a word of the Lord to bring healing he shares it in a user-friendly way so as not to scare guests.

Biblical and pastoral counseling can bring healing and comfort to the inner being. But when God gives revelation knowledge about their condition He can use one prophetic flow to discern the root cause of a problem and speak an anointed word that brings immediate tears and deliverance to set the person free immediately and permanently. God brings personal pictures or words of knowledge about people's situations that bring immediate healing.

A woman in Vermont who had cancer had a vision that she should call our Hershey Medical Center team for healing prayer. God told her to eat chocolate for her healing. She called me and said she would do whatever we said to get her healing. She would come and have us pray over her, whatever we said. We prayed in the chapel for wisdom for what she should do, and God gave the prescription—she will be healed by *great grace*. We got her a Hershey chocolate bar, prayed over it, and sent it to her like it was a healing cloth. We put with it the prescription that she was healed by God's *great grace*. She took the chocolate to her prayer team and they ate it together like they were taking communion.

Then she let the word *great grace* sink into her being. Soon after that, her end-stage cancer diagnosis was changed to cancer-free. The *rhema* word of God sunk into her body, mind, and spirit and brought a transformation that yielded her healing.

Another woman was concerned for her mother's life in the ICU. She asked for prayer in the chapel, and God's word to her was, "It will be OK. I am with you." She didn't know if her mother would live or die, but she had the assurance from the word that God would take care of it and it would be OK. Her mother did die, and she had a peace that it was in God's hands.

Families came for prayer from the children's cancer unit. They had become friends in the children's unit and wanted prayer together. One mother had deep faith for her son's healing. Our team had a sense that her faith would be a beachhead to the other mothers for their faith to bring healing. All three sons had terminal diagnoses. We noted in our prayers that they would be a strength to each other and their sons would live. The two mothers whose faith was strengthened in the healing process saw their sons healed and their families turned to God in the process. But the mother who already had faith lost her son to cancer. She maintained her faith in God and was a continued witness to the other families as she battled the loss of her son with steadfast faith in God. *"I consider that our present sufferings are not worth comparing with the glory that will be revealed in us"* (Rom. 8:18 NIV). Her suffering is great, but the glory is greater in others seeing God move through her life testimony. God is good even in the midst of her trials.

Our team spoke words of life over the three couples holding their three sons in the chapel. Two received physical life and the third went to Heaven but had eternal life. That was hard to understand what God was doing, but we know His character is to be good to His people. And we have to trust in that.

More can be accomplished by a *rhema* word of God to deliver or heal them when God speaks to the root issues in their lives. Bitter roots uncovered can bring healing of crippling effects. Joy applied to depression when the bones have been drying up can restore blood flow and bring oxygenation and nutrients to the joints when the stress and tension is lifted off their mind and cardiovascular system.

Personal words come from God for that individual; they are not *logos* words that you just believe. The mother whose son died had gotten a word that he would live and not die. This word came out of the prayer minister's belief in the Word of God that none would perish. Her heart wanted to give a comforting word to the mother. But a word like, "Your son will live," gives hope to the mom that he will be healed of cancer. Because of his faith in God, he is living with Jesus in Heaven, but the parents have more grief to bear, having thought God said he would live. We have to be careful to not give words about life and death unless they truly are clear words from God for their lives.

Faith does come by hearing the Word. Reading Scripture as truth to sick people and their families brings great strength and healing in their lives. The gifts of the Spirit flowing in the chapel accomplish more in changed lives in five minutes than some can in a series of counseling or medical visits, because the Creator of their being is speaking a word of knowledge from what He knows to be a true source.

A woman was diagnosed with temporomandibular joint pain, which was resulting in ongoing pain and swelling in her jaw. She asked my husband for a second opinion since her problem was not healing. He prayed for God's revelation of the root of the problem, recognizing the symptoms didn't match the diagnosis. He told her to get scans of her jaw, and that became key wisdom for the doctors to find a large tumor that was the real cause of the problem. Incorporating revelation knowledge from God with medical or counseling knowledge brings the best partnership and the greatest healing benefit.

Love Immunity

Jesus offered Himself up in love for us. So we can gather together as brethren to receive His love. Paul warned the Corinthians that many became sick and weak and some died prematurely because saints were not discerning Christ's Body properly (see 1 Cor. 11:29-30). Jesus' banner of love presides over us like His banqueting table of love. He surrounds us and protects us with the immunity of His love which is our immune system individually and corporately. We learn to overcome as we rest in His love, bringing overcoming power and strength. Like Peter walking on the water, we step without crutches. As we do, the pain is gone and we realize we can walk. Walking in faith begins the healing process.

A blind man came to the chapel in desperation because his heart was failing him and he needed to find some peace about dying. Though a Jewish man, he stepped out in faith to reach out for help from God to overcome his fear of death itself. With the prayer team surrounding him, the blind man stretched out his hands to feel around him. He wanted to see who was there. As we told him about our prayer team ready to help him, he began to share his fear of his failing heart that had already had ten heart attacks. Doctors said he would never leave the hospital because of his worn-out heart. He was filled with fear and apparently lived with much fear his whole life. But in the atmosphere of love, we offered him assurance that he could know he would be in Heaven with Jesus.

He said, "Well, I can't do that because I am a Jew and my father is a well-known rabbi."

We said he wouldn't have to leave his Jewish heritage. He would only find the Messiah his people have been looking for all these years. He would have an assurance if he put his faith in Jesus, who came back after He died to show He had power over life and death. This man could open the eyes of his heart to see that Jesus had come as his Savior and did have eternal life for him.

The Jewish man said, "I'll try it. I'll try anything. I have to get peace." So we led him in a salvation prayer, and we prayed a spirit of peace to come over him as God opened his eyes to see his Savior. To his surprise, as he spoke his faith in Jesus to be his Savior, his eyes began to clear and he could see us. He squinted hard and started to describe what he began to see. "Do you have dark hair?" he began.

"Yes, I do!" I shouted, an eager prayer minister.

"Do you have a book in your hand?"

"Yes! It is the Bible!"

Then he exclaimed boldly, "I was blind and now I see. The darkness is gone and now I see the light! And now I feel a peace that I never felt in my 60 years. Wow! I am a new man!" We all rejoiced as we saw his nurse come to get him in his wheelchair and take him back to his room. He kept declaring to her, "I can see now. I was blind and now I see."

Behold the Lord and His love for you. Rejoice as you come to the banqueting presence of God where you experience His healing love. Jesus said that healing is the children's bread (see Matt. 15:25-27). What did He mean? It was a daily experience for Him. And it is a regular experience at God's altar in the medical center. When we come to Him, He is faithful to forgive us our sins and heal us!

The Healing Touch—Believing Prayers

This touch of faith inspires faith in people coming to the chapel. When we extend the touch of faith it builds faith and opens hearts, and they respond to God and their bodies get a healing response.

"Do not be afraid; only believe, and she will be made well" (Luke 8:50). When Jesus spoke to the girl her spirit returned when the belief was lifted. Belief arose, and the girl arose. The authority for ministry flows as faith arises. It ministers to our human hurt and changes us from *dis*ease to *ease*—peace in the Lord.

"Why are you cast down, O my soul?" (Ps. 42:11). Get over it! Put your hope in God and fulfill His purposes.

The Gospel thrives when power and authority are increased. They are increased as we take our eyes off our sickness and suffering and remember the goodness of the Lord in the land of the living. When we expect victory over the powers of darkness or words spoken in discouragement, we shift our thoughts to the goodness of the Lord and His health benefits and suddenly our spirit is lifted. The joy of the Lord becomes our strength, and we are healed even of our emotional distresses, like clinical depression. Luke 10:19 reminds us that we are assigned to do the Lord's business until He returns, and He supplies us with peace and power. So let's get over our depressions and sicknesses and be about the Lord's purposes on the earth.

Be Empowered by God

Divine healing has *dominion* over sickness. It comes as we pray believing prayers. We have authority in prayer, teaching, and personal ministry as we *believe!* There is a dominion in the soul of the person who touches Heaven with his belief. We pray until there is a satisfaction in our souls that the healing prayer is complete. John G. Lake had an X-ray machine in his healing rooms. He wanted to show the dominion of God while he prayed for a man with tuberculosis. Each time they ministered to him in prayer they would take an X-ray of his lungs to show the effects of the prayer. He claimed one could see the progress of healing. Each time they prayed they saw the effects diminish until there was no more tuberculosis.[3] John G. Lake wanted to show the effects of the Holy Spirit on the brain. He allowed doctors to record EEG results as he spoke in tongues and read Psalms 23. *Doctors were amazed, saying that his brain had wider mental range than any other person that they had recorded.*[4]

He went on to show how the Holy Spirit moves on a cellular level as people pray for healing. He showed that the spirit invades the body's cellular structure and brings about the healing effects. He also had doctors record the effects when he laid his hand on a man to bring healing to his leg. Doctors didn't want him to pray for people who had the bubonic plague. But he convinced them that the power of God was stronger than the germs and that His Spirit impacted them more than their disease impacted him.

Jesus told the woman with the issue of blood who reached for His cloak after being to many doctors but not being healed, *"…Your faith has made you well. Go in peace"* (see Luke 8:48). John G. Lake was interacting with doctors in the hospital during the time of the bubonic plague. Doctors told him, "Please stay away or you will get sick."

But John G. Lake said, "No, you will see that when I pray the germs won't jump onto me; the prayers will cause the germs to retreat." He had them do tests to see that his words were true. And they saw the power of the healing prayer to cause sickness to retreat.

Healing grace does transform the souls of humans. The grace removes the effects of sin on the human soul and leaves them to heal from those effects. It gives them strength instead of human weakness and allows the body to rebuild to again be able to fight sickness.

Concerns About Healing in a Medical Setting

Prayer ministers should know that medical staff generally appreciate prayer support for their patients and will give time for prayer over patients, but be aware of the following concerns of medical staff and cooperate with medical recommendations, knowing that doctors will see and document unexpected healings from their medical tests and observations:

1. Doctors are concerned that prayer ministers will give unfounded hope to patients and they won't face the realities of their disease. If our prayers focus on Jesus and his help, hope will not be unfounded and will not disappoint.
2. They are also concerned that prayer ministers will tell patients not to take their medications or cooperate with medical treatment when they need it.
3. Doctors want families to agree to stop life support if the doctor deems it necessary.

Dee, a woman of great faith, asked for prayer for her mother suffering from an infection that invaded her body. Dee did everything she could to pray and care for her mother. She asked our team to pray, and God seemed to be saying, "It'll be OK." We didn't know if that meant her mother would live or die.

Her sisters traveled to do prayer vigil at the bedside. A couple days later, a man came up to Dee in church and said, "God called me to go to your mother's bedside and wash her feet with you today."

So the man she didn't know came with her to the hospital. He stood with her by her mother's side. The man knelt at the bottom of her mother's hospital bed and washed her mother's feet and prayed for her. Then he stood behind Dee and said he would hold her with Jesus' arms to comfort her if she wanted. She watched her mother and let him hold her as she trembled, knowing her mother was slipping away. He said, "If you look up you can see the angels coming to get her. God will show you."

She looked up and saw bright sparkly lights above her mother's bed. It seemed so holy. Then they disappeared. He said, "God will only show it to you for a brief moment." Dee was at perfect peace like in a fairy tale dream. Then the man said he would go now.

After he walked out of the room, the nurse said, "Her vital signs are dropping now." So Dee called the man back, and together they took the last breaths with her mom. Dee knew the angels had taken her to be with Jesus, and Dee knew it would be OK, just as God spoke the first time we met and prayed.

Dee did not expect to lose her mom. She prayed for healing, but God met her in such a peaceful way. He was with her in such a tangible way that she remembers His presence and remembers her mother's passing on to be a beautiful experience.

Hedge of Protection

There is a powerful shelter and defensive wall the Lord builds around His people. Isaiah 22:8 refers to it. Things that help to provide a strong protective wall around us are angels, prosperity, prayer warriors, prophetic words, property, provision, and good relationships. The story of Job and God's removal of his hedge for divine testing is an example of the vulnerability of not having the hedge in place. The believer's hedge is made up of goodness, righteousness, sowing, reaping, and a pure, forgiving heart. Guardian angels are dispatched by God over a believer's life. Elisha had a spiritual hedge of protection, as seen in Second Kings 6:17.

A broken hedge is a situation where a person's life is vulnerable to the enemy to come and plunder that life. The absence of prayers, prophetic impact, impartation, pastorship, personal economy, and employment viability are all contributing factors. Adding rejection of God, backsliding, disobedience, and rebellion can cause the hedge to be broken or dissolved. Idolatry always deteriorates a hedge around a life. But as with Job, God can allow it to be broken to affirm allegiance to Him, and it can bring glory to Him to restore it manifold at the end of a test period.

Pray Psalms 91 as a divine protection over the prayer team and ministry. Psalms 91 is important to pray over all prayer ministers and their families as God's angelic protection over us. Pray it for four categories of help from God:

1. *Divine Protection*—He is our refuge and fortress (Psalms 91:1-2).
2. *Divine Providence*—He will deliver and cover us (Psalms 91:3-8).
3. *Divine Reward*—we are assured He will send guardian angels (Psalms 91:9-13).
4. *Divine Promise*—His love is set upon us that we have the blessings of deliverance, answered prayer, long life, and victory (Psalms 91:14-16).

The Bronze Serpent

The bronze serpent was made by Moses at the direction of the Lord Himself.

> *Therefore the people came to Moses, and said, "We have sinned, for we have spoken against the Lord and against you; pray to the Lord that He take away the serpents from*

> *us." So Moses prayed for the people. Then the Lord said to Moses, "Make a fiery serpent, and set it on a pole; and it shall be that everyone who is bitten, when he looks at it, shall live." So Moses made a bronze serpent, and put it on a pole; and so it was, if a serpent had bitten anyone, when he looked at the bronze serpent, he lived* (Numbers 21:7-9).

The Israelites were near the end of their 40-year wilderness journey. Instead of thanking the Lord for delivering them from slavery in Egypt and caring for them for 40 years in the wilderness, they complained and questioned God's motives. "Why have you brought us out of Egypt to die in the desert? Why is there no bread or water?" They were dissatisfied with God's provision. How could they be so callous to God's provision? As the people complained, God sent poisonous snakes as punishment, but He provided a bronze serpent on a pole so they could look upon the serpent of bronze and live.

Their suffering was a result of their rebellion against both God and Moses. They even despised the manna God gave them in the desert. In essence, they were rejecting God's provision for life. The snakes ended up provoking repentance in the people and an appeal to pray to God on their behalf. This illustrates the power of intercessory prayer. Moses' prayer prevailed to set aside the punishment, even though the people had brought it upon themselves by rejecting the promise and preferring a life of slavery. God generally used means understood by the people of the time.

Why a bronze serpent? God chose this unusual method to bring healing to his dying people because John 3 tells us that the bronze serpent lifted on a pole is a picture of lifting Jesus on the Cross for our salvation from sin once and for all.

> *And as Moses lifted up the serpent in the wilderness, even so must the Son of Man be lifted up, that whoever believes*

in Him should not perish but have eternal life. For God so loved the world that He gave His only begotten Son, that whoever believes in Him should not perish but have everlasting life (John 3:14-16).

The story of the bronze serpent crafted of dark, inferior metal was the image of healing from the curse of sin. The idea was that the serpent was the cause of all sickness, which was a direct result of the sin of humanity. And that the causes were as old and crude as the original sinner. Moses was instructed to prepare this in the wilderness. The bronze serpent is the symbol of the medical industry. When Moses erected it, people were to gaze upon it and find their healing from the death of the serpent bite.

The bronze snake is a *figure of Christ* who is lifted up for our cure. Like a fountain of life springing up, this is a healing well watering the people in a dry desert, refreshing and reviving them with the loving God.

Healing waters are released when we lift our eyes to Jesus. When He is lifted up for all to see, the healing fountain will flow.

Endnotes

1. Henry W. Wright, *A More Excellent Way: Be In Health* (Thomaston, GA: Pleasant Valley Church, 2005), 13.

2. Lord Alfred Tennyson, "The Coming of Arthur," in the *Idylls of the King,* published 1859. Available at http://www. britannia.com/history/idylls.html.

3. Kenneth Copeland, *John G. Lake: His Life, His Sermons, His Boldness of Faith* (Fort Worth, TX: Kenneth Copeland Publications, 1995), 263.

4. Ibid., 305.

Chapter 7

Womb of Healing
to the Nations

God has shown us repeatedly that this chapel is a womb of healing to the nations. God demonstrates His sovereignty even in the core team He picked to lead the ministry. As the pastoral leader of the ministry, I was diagnosed 35 years ago with endometrial cancer, and I was told I would never have children. My imaginations brought me fear for my life and that I could never have a family. Then I decided to go for prayer and anointing for healing with the elders of my church. One of the elders was a physician at the medical center. The compassion of Christ came upon him as he prayed and anointed me, and I could tell the Spirit of God was moving in him and that I was being healed. His was clearly a fervent prayer of a righteous man.

That next year I got married, and two years later we had our first child. I praised God for her life and prayed God would make her little life a light that the world would see. I prayed she would have a voice that would be heard around the world. She grew to become a radio personality on a Christian radio station, and her voice is now heard around the world on the Internet. She did have a learning disability known as attention deficit hyperactivity disorder, which was a struggle in her school days. But it turned out to be a gift to her radio career, as she could multitask and speak energetically at the same time, doing her programming and talking simultaneously. The hyperactivity turned out to be a gift to make her an entertaining and skilled broadcaster. We had three more children who are all strong in faith and impacting others in testimony for God through their lives.

My physical womb, which was diagnosed to never bear a child, bore four children, and then I jokingly asked God to stop as four seemed to be enough. God used a woman diagnosed to be barren to be healed and bear children in the natural to lead a ministry to impact the world. And I was also to lead a healing ministry in the chapel of the hospital where I received my healing from a physician. I now lead a ministry that is called to be a womb of healing to the nations. Our firstborn son was born with the cord wrapped around his neck three times and was blue when he was delivered. God answered a quick prayer for him and breath was restored. He now believes his life was spared for a purpose—to take a message to the world through media.

Three of our dedicated prayer ministers were born prematurely with their lives in the balance. One was born to a mother who died through complications from childbirth. She was orphaned at birth. Two of our prayer team are house parents in the Milton Hershey School and have hearts to heal the children. Another team member lost a child at the medical center and wants to help young parents whose children are suffering. These sufferings in our lives have bonded our hearts to be compelled to pray for the sick and suffering needs in the hospital. God uses miseries and turns them to ministries. Though we don't understand in the moment of suffering in our lives what is happening, God does have His purpose that we will see in years to come.

When I told my father of the healing of my womb he said, "Of course you would be healed. Your grandmother was miraculously healed of a stroke when she was unable to talk and unable to use her left arm and leg. The family called for a pastor to anoint her for healing and she was completely healed by the next day." Dad said there was a healing heritage in my family's spiritual DNA, and my family history was filled with doctors and pastors.

There is a spiritual heritage that we carry with blessings that come from prayers of generations past that strengthen the call on our lives. There is a family well of prayer that has been lifted up that contributes to the ministry we have today. Honor your fathers and the blessings they carry to benefit from the spiritual inheritance in your heritage. My heritage went back to Germany, which was called to be a Fatherland, though Hitler misused that loving Father call to be a controlling father figure. The womb of healing is a womb of restoring the Father's love and healing grace on people's lives.

A womb is a protective, secluded space where things are conceived and formed. It is a place of incubation. It brings forth new life. Seeds of life are conceived into new life and grow in the protective environment until they are ready for new birth in the world. The chapel is the center where all people are welcome to come to God for the needs on their hearts. People need God's help when their need is beyond what medical care can do. People get connected to God in a deeper way at their point of need. And people of all faiths are delighted to find a team that has God's compassion for their need.

The chapel is also a place Muslims use as their altar to Allah and the Jews use as their place of prayer. Our prayer time, being noon to one, ends before the Muslims come for their Friday prayers. They hear our prayers and praises of healings and are surprised at the different prayers we pray. A woman would come for her prayers during our service and be surprised to note people praising God for healings as a result of prayer. She had a prayer need for her husband and was surprised to find the prayer answered. She came back to tell us her prayer was answered and how God hears our prayers.

Different Muslim people come from other nations. An Indian pastor came in to pray for his orphanages, for young girls in danger of being sold as prostitutes. A Liberian pastor came in and was so moved by the prayer ministry that he wanted to start it in Liberia. All people of all nations are touched by the love and healing prayers. The personal touch of the love of God is a life-changing touch on their hearts and spirits. They want it for their families and people back home. Once one man gets a touch, he brings his family back to experience it. Whether they are sick or not, they want a touch from God. He is birthing healing of people of all nations as they recognize the personal love of God. Religion doesn't offer that, but the humble touch of God ministers deep.

Most people are moved to tears in the presence of God in the loving atmosphere of the womb of healing, and it births something in their lives that they take back to their families and friends. In most cases, patients are too sick to come to the chapel, but their families get a touch and then take the healing touch back to their own family members. It is a sweet transfer of the love of God that spreads from one family to another, building the family of God. This womb of healing is birthing a multitude through many who are imparted the love of God to take back to their own.

Renewal of the Mind and Heart

Spiritual transformation comes with the renewal of the mind. New peace and life come as new spiritual insights are discovered to bring new life and health. Families come to the chapel after getting devastating prognoses from their doctors. They come out of desperation because they need help from God to cope with what they have heard. Then, in the meditative healing atmosphere, the burden of it seems to lift and they get new hope in God. It is a mind-transforming experience as they are lifted from despair to hope and trust that God will be with them in it. God is our refuge and help in times of need. He is the holy Comforter and Healer of body, soul, and spirit. Their minds are filled with new hope in the greatest physician, Jehovah Rapha. They realize new ways to pray. They can submit to the report of the doctor, and they can appeal to God for help and listen for the report of the Lord.

A 60-year-old man came to the chapel with repeated heart attacks and a fear of what would happen to him. Doctors told him he wouldn't ever leave the hospital, and he feared what was coming. Having much heartache in his life, he had multiple heart attacks causing irreparable damage to his heart. Openly sharing his fears with our team, we told him there was a way he could have peace with God and assurance of where he would go after he died. With no other option, he agreed to pray to Jesus to save him from death and give him eternal life. As soon as he prayed that prayer, a spirit of peace came over him that amazed him, as he never experienced it before. In one prayer of abandonment to God, his emotional and spiritual heart was healed and he suddenly had a new joy. The salvation prayer healed his spirit and soul, and doctors later saw his physical heart strengthened so he could return home after all.

Believing Across the Miles

One week we had a profound healing prayer time for a woman named Sue. She was in surgery in another hospital in another state to remove a rapidly spreading cancerous tumor the size of a tangerine in her jaw. The Lord gave a picture as the team prayed for Sue's surgery on her jaw—our prayers were extending golden healing hands toward Sue across the miles while she was in the surgery. When the surgery ended Sue's husband called with devastating news. The doctors could not remove all the rapidly growing tumor and they had no other solution to stop its rapid growth. They had already done radiation and that didn't stop its growth. He said she only had a few months to live. Her husband was distraught that nothing more could save his wife.

This news surprised me because our prayers had revealed a picture of healing hands releasing healing during the surgery. So, in bolstered faith, we said we would believe the report of the Lord. Sue's husband was so encouraged by that report that he put the phone to Sue's ear in the recovery room and had me tell her what happened while we prayed during her surgery. We kept praying what the Lord had shown us as Sue recovered. Sue continued to go through the medical scans to observe the tumor. She had a sense she had been healed and her jaw was feeling much better, and to the surprise of the doctors the tumor dissipated. Soon it was gone, puzzling the doctors as they looked at her scans. They had no explanation except to say there must have been a divine intervention. Still baffled by the healing, they insisted on frequent scans to watch for a recurrence. Sue cooperated with the treatments, believing God would verify through the doctor's report the healing He had done to restore her life. And she continues to be in cancer-free health!

Our prayers can impact people around the world. An Iraqi leader emailed me of his hospitalization and serious illness. I sent an email that I would pray for his healing, and that night he said Jesus and I appeared to him by his bedside and told him he would be healed. The next day he was well and discharged from the hospital. Jesus demonstrated his love and kingdom power to that man who became a believer.

Chapter 8

Ministers Taking Healing
to the Nations

*For this reason, they are before the throne of God; and they
serve Him day and night in His temple; and He who sits on
the throne will spread His tabernacle over them. ...for the
Lamb in the center of the throne will be their shepherd, and will
guide them to springs of the water of life; and God will wipe
every tear from their eyes* (Revelation 7:15,17 NASB).

After the Amish school shootings, families throughout the
Amish community were reeling with how to cope with the
tragedy. They had been a peaceable community, and this type of
tragedy had not struck their community before, so they had no
experience with how to handle it. I was part of a team called to
minister to some Amish families collected in a barn. We sang
some worship songs, prayed, and sought God's help in the tragedy. As we prayed, the presence of God came and ministered wisdom and revelation to the families and their children suffering

with the trauma of the injury and loss of their friends. God empowered them with prayers that miraculously sustained the life of a girl friend of a girl there. God established His glory among them, and they called the barn a glory barn as they prayed to the Lord in it. This was an emergency wellspring set up for healing in the face of crisis.

Taking God to the nations is extending His Kingdom love as a model to the nations. God's Kingdom penetrates societies around the earth, breathing healing life and wholeness to the nations. It provides relevant healing help as it brings the Gospel to the people around the earth in their time of healing need. And it brings needed reconciliation to the people who were intended to dwell peaceably with one another. It helps them to return to the Creator and Sustainer of abundant life and realize their need for His healing, redeeming love.

Revelation speaks of the river of life that flows from the throne of God to bring healing life in every season, the leaves of the tree drawing sustenance from the healing waters (see Rev. 22:2). Isaiah speaks of people as trees that have been battered through the oppressions of life to rise up to be strong oaks of righteousness (see Isa. 61:3-4).

Hosting wellsprings around the world brings a protective covering of the presence of God over people of the earth. With the acceleration of troublesome times in the earth, people will run to these wellsprings for living fountains of waters to revive them. The Spirit of God will draw them to these wellsprings wherever we establish our places of prayer as prayer altars to worship Him.

Just as ancient wells have always brought refreshing waters in the desert, so are wellsprings refreshing to people's spirits everywhere. Wells were historically the place to get life-giving water, and they were the congregating place of people in the towns as people came to draw the water for their households. The well at Sychar was where Jesus met the Samaritan woman when she came to draw life-sustaining water for her household. But Jesus offered her an eternal drink of living water that would never make her thirst again. It would be so satisfying to her soul that she would not thirst for earthly satisfaction in wrong relationships. It would bring satisfaction to her lifelong inner longings. He offered her a soul satisfaction she looked for in many relationships but could only get by coming to Him. And she realized it as soon as He spoke His understanding of her life and offered His eternal gift to her personally.

Ancient wells were dug deep through bedrock until they reached a level of flowing water that would gush to refresh and provide a never-ending, satisfying supply. That is what people find at the well of God's presence. People all around the world have a thirst for this deep, eternal wellspring for their soul satisfaction. No matter what religion they follow, everyone longs to have that inner peace with the living God and to be able to say, "It is well with my soul." They will be like the man with the damaged heart who came to the medical center well and finally, at 60 years old, found the peace he was looking for all his life and the resultant spontaneous healing to his physical eyes and heart. People long for this experience at a living well.

First Nations chief Ivan Doxtator believes the First Nations people still have the spiritual authority over the land, and until they are honored the healing will not flow for America, not until these relationships are recognized with government apologies and aid. Senator Brownback has introduced this legislation nationally, and Senator Greenleaf has passed an apology from the Pennsylvania Senate. The bedrock that the United States and other nations have to dig deep through is these ancient relationships that need restoration between the First Nations people and the white people. This model of healing and restoration of the first relationships in the land is needed around the world to bring forth the life-giving wellsprings and restored relationships. Father God has loved each people group with an everlasting love that will release healing when they recognize it. Even the sons of Abraham and the nations that have proceeded from Isaac and Ishmael need to bring healing to the tribes of nations that make up the family of God.

> *If My people who are called by My name will humble themselves, and pray and seek My face, and turn from their wicked ways, then I will hear from Heaven, and will forgive their sin and heal their land* (2 Chronicles 7:14).

Prayer by itself does not get the job done for healing to spring forth. We need to meet God's requirements for healing in the land, in our families, and in our personal lives. God is speaking about a nation receiving healing, and He requires the people to humble themselves and pray to Him. But He says He won't listen from Heaven until they turn from their wicked ways. They need to turn from devotion to other idols or ungodly behaviors that separate them from communion with the true God. This will release healing to their nation. Then He will advance His Kingdom, forgiving their sin and healing their land, causing it to be fertile and flourish.

The personal healing prescription from Jehovah Rapha can also be applied to healing of nations.

> *Is anyone* [any nation] *among you sick? Let him* [the nation] *call for the elders of the church, and let them pray over him* [the nation], *anointing him with oil in the name of the Lord. And the prayer of faith will save the sick, and the Lord will raise him* [the nation] *up. And if he* [the nation] *has committed sins, he will be forgiven* (James 5:14-15).

God entrusts the faithful leaders of the church to release healing in the people and in the land. God's principle is that He looks among nations for a person to stand in the gap. Daniel modeled this when he repented for his own nation. He prayed:

> *O Lord, great and awesome God, who keeps His covenant and mercy with those who love Him, and with those who keep His commandments, we have sinned and committed iniquity, we have done wickedly and rebelled, even by departing from Your precepts and Your judgments. Neither have we heeded Your servants the prophets, who spoke in Your name.... As it is written in the Law of Moses, all this disaster has come upon us; yet we have not made our prayer before the Lord our God, that we might turn from our iniquities and understand Your truth. ...Now therefore, our God, hear the prayer of Your servant, and his supplications, and for the Lord's sake cause Your face to shine on Your sanctuary, which is desolate* (Daniel 9:4-6,13,17).

We need to pray and contend for God's favor so we can be vessels for His noble use, bringing healing blessings to cities and nations of the world.

Restorative Plan of Jesus' Ministry

1. *The anointed one brings salvation and healing.* The anointed one shares the good news of God's love by preaching, healing, and setting people free. He is a healer and messenger of freedom and comfort. This is the essence of Jesus' ministry but also the ministry He passes on to the Church.
2. *Everlasting joy springs forth.* The oil of joy and gladness turn mourning and suffering into the planting of the Lord. They rise up to be strong, righteous oak trees that become pillars in the Kingdom of God.

3. *Everlasting covenants are restored.* People become priests for the nations, honoring God's purposes, and righteousness springs forth before all the nations.

God is a covenant-keeping God, and He will redeem His covenants established with humanity at the beginning of time. He uses healing to demonstrate His love, and He restores His people, turning their times of mourning into dancing and giving the everlasting joy of the Lord. The Kurdish people know that full well as they literally dance on the mountainside of the land where their people were slain by their own leadership regime. They know the healing victory of God, taking the difficult seasons in their lives as training grounds to bring inner strength that cannot be shaken.

We become like the strongest, oaks of righteousness, like the planting of the Lord, Isaiah 61:3 after our times of suffering. God does a mighty inner strengthening as we struggle through hard times. Joseph said to his brothers, *"You intended to harm me, but God intended it for good to accomplish what is now being done, the saving of many lives"* (Gen. 50:20 NIV). The Lord's intention was in the evil strategy of his brothers, but God redeemed it to set Joseph high in Pharaoh's court to move on that level of leadership. The message is strong. The Lord uses trials to build an inner strength in us for greater leadership in His Kingdom.

God uses earthquakes and natural disasters to bring supernatural results. These become times of awakening to our need for God, and His loving, rescuing response shakes people with reminders of His coming Kingdom. During the aftershock of 9/11, people roamed the streets in shock singing worship to God, and word spread across the nation: "God Bless America." People get shaken back into the reality of our need to get back to God and this releases healing benefits to our people and our land.

The City Is Made Glad

God is our refuge and strength, a very present help in trouble…there is a river whose streams shall make glad the city of God (Psalms 46:1,4).

It becomes a sanctuary of the Most High God. Though the nations rage and wars and desolations can be around us, we have a refuge in the Lord that is a present help. Just as Jerusalem has a subterranean water supply that is the source of fountains and pools in the city, the unseen river becomes an unseen source of bubbling fountains. So is the Spirit of God flowing through the human spirit to be a wellspring of wisdom and healing life. It overflows out of a revived person's life like a fountainhead of life-giving water.

This was witnessed in the life of the Samaritan woman who came to draw water from the well and encountered Jesus. She was a social outcast, living as a woman of ill repute with multiple husbands, but Jesus didn't rebuke her for it. He simply let her know He knew it and He had a life-giving spiritual water to offer her. Receiving His edifying words, she ran from the well to tell all in her city, and her testimony made the whole city glad and believe in the life-giving God.

The fruit of the testimony of one life revived and filled with overflowing gladness makes others glad as they hear. It becomes a naturally supernatural outflow of the healing love of God to others as one person shares their testimony of healing with another. When people in the medical setting hear this good news from "God testimonies" while their lives are in calamity, it becomes life-giving news that makes them glad at the goodness of the Lord, and they believe He can heal them, too. The ministries of the Lord go forth with the emotional fruits of the spirit—love, joy, peace, patience, kindness, goodness, faith (see Gal. 5:22-23).

Once people have God minister to them, they rejoice and go and tell others. It builds a city of increasing faith which causes the naturally supernatural healings to increase in the community.

Joy to the World

As we seek the fullness of the Lord, His presence fills us and the places we dwell. The Lord is our strength and power. A new song of victory springs forth from our lives. As we learn to live deeper and deeper in His presence, He takes us higher and higher into His heavenly atmosphere, impacting our lives and health. We walk a new walk. Our cellular bodies are revived and restored. We sing with a new joy that truly is our strength. The Lord has done great things, and to Him we are eternally grateful. Our focus is on the goodness of the Lord in the land of the living. And we are living with new life and bounce in our steps. We know deep in our hearts He has gained the victory, and we delight in it as joy of His Kingdom bubbles up and overflows out of us.

No matter the depths of pain and suffering we have experienced, new life sprouts out of us. We find ourselves dwelling in the tree of life by the streams of living water, and we know the assurance of life forevermore with our King of kings. We delight in Him and His victories in our lives. And He delights in us that we have come to a strengthened place of overcoming sufferings in our lives, bringing new life wherever we go. We can truly break forth in new song. He has birthed a great thing in us and in the world. The sunrise has arisen in us and we find we have healing in our wings and we can soar above the struggles of life.

As a young woman, I had many dreams of being able to flap my arms and fly above the problems of life. Whenever I encountered insurmountable obstacles I would delight in arising above them and watching down on them from a perspective on high. I would enjoy the freedom in being able to rise up above any struggle and see from God's perspective.

Forefathers' Faith

> *...I will preserve You and give You as a covenant to the people, to restore the earth, to cause them to inherit the desolate heritages...He who has mercy on them will lead them, even by the springs of water He will guide them* (Isaiah 49:8,10).

There is a renewal coming from the deep heritage of the Lord. Covenantal roots laid deep in the soil of our land are being watered by prayers from deep springs of faith. The Lord says, *"In an acceptable time I have heard You, and in the day of salvation I have helped You..."* (Isa. 49:8). We are in the acceptable timing of the Lord that covenantal roots are being exposed and refreshed as praying people are awakening to realize these purposes still need to come forth. God will awaken the church first and their renewed strength will bring a tidal force wave of evangelism as it restores the covenantal foundations.

When we get discouraged by the issues and problems in the world today we need to draw deep on the faith of the fathers of our faith. Abraham was the founding father of our faith. A cloud of witnesses came after him. We know the promises of God and we know many are living testimonies that God's words are true and bear witness in people's lives. The word of their living testimonies gives us faith to believe God at His word. We need to separate our perspective from the things of the world and gain divine perspective. As we realize the holy purposes of God, we find ourselves repenting of even the sins of our nation, and then the refreshing washing of the Word comes. The fruit is seen in a washing and refreshing that comes over our spirits.

> *Repent therefore and be converted, that your sins may be blotted out, so that times of refreshing may come from the presence of the Lord* (Acts 3:19).

"Wash and refresh and draw deeper," says the Lord. "Find times of refreshing in My presence. Let your hearts not be depressed, but sing in My presence." Get your spirits up like the lame man got up. Jesus took him by the hand and lifted him up to get into the waters and fill his legs with healing strength to walk straight and stable, keeping his eyes on Jesus. With each step his faith grew stronger and his heart rejoiced more until he gave a shout of exuberance.

Worship and waiting for God's presence to fill us draws the people to us that are in need. Many are drawn as they hear the soothing music beckoning them in. Worship builds unity of focus in our prayers before the altar of God. Then the Spirit comes on our souls and wonders and signs are done through us like they were the apostles. In the worship we confess anything that blocks the flow of the Spirit through us.

The watering of the Word is being washed by the Word to align our spirits and prayers, reading the Word, and aligning our hearts with the Word and with one another. It means confessing anything we need to make our hearts fertile ground to prepare ourselves to be vessels in ministry.

Walking out victories. A lame man was brought to the apostles. Peter reached out his hand to the lame man's hand and spoke: *"In the name of Jesus Christ* [which means Anointed Savior] *of Nazareth, rise up and walk"* (Acts 3:6).

He took him by the right hand and lifted him up, and immediately his anklebones received strength. So he, leaping up, stood and walked and entered the temple with them, walking and leaping and praising God. Then as the people gathered in amazement Peter said:

> *The God of Abraham, Isaac, and Jacob, the God of our fathers, glorified His Servant Jesus, whom you delivered up and denied in the presence of Pilate, when he was determined to let Him go. But you denied the Holy One and the Just, and asked for a murderer to be granted to you, and killed the Prince of life, whom God raised from the dead, of which we are witnesses. And His name, through faith in His name, has made this man strong, whom you see and know. Yes, the faith which comes through Him has given him this perfect soundness in the presence of you all* (Acts 3:13-16).

Healing in Jesus' name. Healing happened by faith in Jesus' name alone. The anointing of Jesus' name brings the power and authority to heal! We carry that authority to heal by His holy name. And His name is lifted up so that all can see. The healings are signs and wonders for people to see the manifestation of their faith. To see that, truly, the Kingdom of God is at hand. It is at our hands and fingertips! We had a woman who walked for her first time at our gate beautiful and she got a gleeful smile of joy. Her testimony of a life being restored is a living witness to the God in whom we place our faith. So it is not our faith that heals, but faith in Jesus Christ. I believe You, Jesus, that You can heal.

Chapter 9

Healing Arising in the Nations

*The Sun of Righteousness shall arise with healing in His wings...
and he will turn the hearts of the fathers to the children, and
the hearts of the children to the fathers"* (Malachi 4:2,6).

A healing revival is being released throughout the world, where the everlasting heart of God is redeeming the families of the earth back to himself. The blessing of Abraham's Seed Faith is being watered by the redemptive love of God so it can grow and multiply. God told Abraham He had made a covenant with him. *"...And in your seed all the families of the earth shall be blessed"* (Acts 3:25). God's covenantal blessing was not limited to Abraham's Jewish bloodline, but to all the families of the earth. We all can enjoy that covenantal blessing.

Spiritual roots of disease arise from a feeling of separation from God, His approval, and His love. A feeling that God has forsaken or rejected us causes discouragement and susceptibility to many diseases. Generational roots of families in restrictive religions and nations tend to feel guilty by association. They carry an orphaned spirit feeling rejected and cut off from the love of God. They also tend to suffer from depression, addictions, and psychosomatic disease. *"God so loved the world that He gave His only begotten Son, that whoever believes in Him should not perish but have everlasting life"* (John 3:16). This becomes a refreshing healing message to them. Restoration to Father God and His family of believers becomes a healing message that strengthens their body, mind, and spirit and has far-reaching effects in personal healing and community welfare. To come to the medical care center and also find spiritual support brings healing in the fullest sense.

Chapel ministries in medical centers around the world can become a place where God refreshes the faith of people from across the world. What people have in common in that place is their sickness and suffering. Doctors come to a healing well, chaplains come, U.S. representatives come, dying people come, poor people come, Amish people come, Muslims come, Jews come, Catholics come, and Spirit-filled people come. People of all faiths come, but what drives them all to the chapel well is they know they need God's help. The chapel atmosphere anywhere in the earth welcomes them to come sit before God and make their appeal. And His help comes not by might, nor by power, but by the Spirit of God. His overcoming Spirit works though prayer ministers and staff that come together with families of faith from around the world. Discouragement in time of need is overcome by the grace of God ministering through people at the altar. His goodness is seen as joyful stories rise even out of pain and suffering. As long as hearts are turned to Father God in faith, He is there to pour out His loving care to meet them at their point of need.

This work of building a temple of His presence in a public medical center would be by providence and divine grace a faith-filled result, though many come from different faith perspectives.

God will remove barriers as the focus is on Jesus and His restorative healing to our bodies and souls.

Fountain of the Water of Life

There is a spiritual fountain that flows freely. It flows in the medical center chapel. It flows in the Harrisburg capitol; it flows in the deserts of the Middle East. It flows to the nations; it flows from the throne of God. It brings life abundantly wherever it flows. The River of Life feeds the tree of life, which restores life abundantly. God said:

> *I am the Alpha and the Omega, the Beginning and the End. I will give of the fountain of the water of life freely to him who thirsts. He who overcomes shall inherit all things, and I will be his God and He shall be My son* (Revelation 21:6-7).

God is restoring His people and purposes over all the earth. He calls us to return to Him to be cleansed of all sin. He is bringing a purifying, refreshing renewal that would result from our entering His presence. We look to the return of the Bride of Christ, restored in power and purity. Repentance and rest play such key roles in the restoration.

Healing to the nations involves reconciliation between people groups. Intercessors' mediation unites believing remnants to represent nations to do the reconciliatory work, bringing healing to the land.

Power is released when believers intercede in unity and humility. They can even set in motion divided nations to reconcile. Their heart attitude of identification repentance touches the heart of God. Believers become reconcilers before God and in man's relationships. We apply healing balm on ancient wounds.

As members of our prayer team went out to the nations, we noticed sickness in regions related to the environmental issues in those regions. Sicknesses reflected the problems of the area. For example, the men were infertile in a region where there had been radiation from bombing. Or cancer would be high where environmental toxins were in the atmosphere. Children had facial and eye injuries where land mines were prevalent. People had enteritis where water was not pure. Healing prayer and community education and environmental programs can be established to bring healing to the regions.

Revival to the world will come as each nation realizes its God-ordained fruit and gets set free from the ills and oppression that holds it back. As the Sun of Righteousness arises over all the families of the earth there will be a healing, redeeming effect around the world. The Malachi 4 call for the heart of the fathers to return to the children and the hearts of the children to return to the fathers will still be redeemed and will cause a sweeping revival to the families of the earth. When Israel sees the light of the glory of God, the return of the Messiah to Jerusalem will bring the ultimate healing to the land!

Leaders traveling to the nations realize their fruit. Our healing missions to the Middle East revealed a great revival bursting in the people who recognize the fruitfulness of living faith connected to God's heart. When they see the heart of God ministering to their healing needs and other personal needs, they are drawn to the Light of the World. The healing touch of the Lord revives their lives and cities. They are ripe for the Lord's redemptive love.

The Lord said to go into all the world and preach the Gospel, and signs would follow those who believe (see Mark 16:15-17). As our team goes to Mali and just walks among the people, the Lord opens their eyes to see and their ears to hear. The nations will see the Kingdom of God is at hand as they see God's people walk among them with the heart of God.

As we take trips to Iraq, the local leaders see the rains come in the desert and a rainbow the Lord sets in the sky over cities just at the moment that our motorcade enters the city gates. The governmental leaders believe the heavens are opened wherever we go, and we have come as messengers from God who have God's heart for them. Being carriers of the living Jesus impacts the atmosphere and the hearts of the people wherever we go. We set up medical clinics and village outreach with healing prayer along with medical care. They come even if they are well because they want the healing prayers. They sense the true spirit of God over them as we pray, and the spring of living waters run down their cheeks as they are moved by the love of God calling them. Praise the Living God!

Chapter 10

Global House of Healing

Just as houses of prayer are being established all over the world, so are healing chapels. People are recognizing the importance of healing prayer combined with medical care. And they are realizing the benefits of rest, revelation, and restoration in healing of people and nations. As people reawaken to the importance of calming down their busy lives to remember the refreshing Garden of Eden atmosphere that God first established for us to dwell in fellowship with Him, they are realizing the health benefits of entering and enjoying that refreshing, restful relationship with Him. Revelation flows from restored relationship with God as He first established in the Garden. Then, restoration happens for people to know the fullness of God's first mandate to us to be fruitful and multiply and have dominion over all living things. There is a destiny to be fulfilled as humankind is healed and restored to the purposes for which we were first created.

Restoration of God's redemptive love is arising over the nations as more people bow to show honor to God. People all over the world are moved by a personal touch from God and His people. The tabernacle of God is with us. His presence settles every issue. In Him there is no more pain, no more crying; behold, He makes all things new.

The World Needs a Place to Find Healing Rest

Psalms 23 guides us in entering the healing, refreshing rest of the Lord. It begins with, *"The Lord is my shepherd; I shall not want"* (Ps. 23:1). If we truly recognize Him as Lord of our lives we will have no want because He satisfies our heart's deepest desire. To truly enter the Lord's rest is to know the inner peace with which He leads us, and He quiets our soul and restores it beside still waters. To enter His rest is to enter a peaceful confidence in God that we cast aside all concerns. This is a daily restoration from the anxieties of the day, gaining refreshing inner strength. We can have the assurance that we can follow Him in the paths He leads.

The key to provision of all our needs is the presence of God. This leads us to delight in His holy name. Too often we seek Him for our needs to be met, but He actually meets our needs while we delight in Him.

Relaxation is an important key to health and well-being. It is our antidote to stress, which is known to exacerbate illness and disease. When we relax, our body can unwind from the tension in our biological systems. Relaxation calms down our cardiovascular system, giving the heart a rest and reduces our blood pressure. Breathing is slowed down, reducing the need for oxygen. Blood flow is increased to the muscles and muscle tension is reduced. All systems get rest and have renewed energy and enhanced immunity. It clears the mind to be able to focus on healing the body.

The Soul at Rest

There are spiritual benefits of being still before God. An enduring rest and peace can emerge when people learn to sit still in the presence of God through Scripture, praying, meditation, and listening prayer. These are forms of prayer listed in Scripture that bring inner peace and rest. They cause the body to calm down and align with the Spirit of God. Even cells are alerted to spiritual alignment with God that causes balance in the body and releases blood flow to nourish the cells for healing.

Discover contemplative prayer. David was called a man after God's heart. He was a man that could worship in his inner being with such peace that he could go before the king and his radical emotions and calm the heart of the king. David was a shepherd who understood the meaning of his words, *"The Lord is my shepherd; I shall not want"* (Ps. 23:1). He knew deep inner peace that he imparted to the heart of the king as he played his harp. Meditation lays the groundwork for deep and searching communion with God. We become still and listen for the still, small voice that is ready to meet us as we seek Him out. Revelation says there is a door open, and God invites us to come up to Him (see Rev. 4:1).

There is a promise of rest if we enter the rest, but the rest does not abide in their spirits unless they have fertile hearts of faith to receive it deep in their being. A daughter of a dying woman brought this poem to the chapel ministry as her gift to others who might be struggling as well.

Burdens Lifting

Love more, obey more

"Come to Me. Come to Me unafraid.
Rest in My love. Touch My hands and feel the peace
passing from Me to you. Come closer.

Sit by Me. Stay by Me and rest.
Give Me all you have. Release the tightness in your heart.
Release it. Think of all the ways in which you have seen Me.
Feel all the warmth where you have felt Me...and release.
This is another way of praying, of communion
with Me. Hear Me...unafraid.

Receive Me...accept My words... My will.
Keep your mind clear; keep your stance firm.
Love, obey, receive the blessings.

Love more, obey more, receive more blessings.
They are out there for you. Just claim them, take them,
enjoy them. I need you strong and undoubtedly Mine.
It is Me, the Father. The one who creates the
minimum feeling, the maximum strength.

It is Me and all is well."

(author unknown)

A woman was getting daily radiation treatments and sensed God wanted her to come to the medical center for her treatments. She came daily for treatments and then found out about our prayer time. Then she started coming every Friday for prayer, but she had a somber appearance about her. She carried much grief about changes in her life and needed the prayers to lift her grief off of her and fill her with the joy of God. As soon as we showed that support, her visage changed and she seemed happier.

Another woman came in, very frightened for her husband whose lung had collapsed and he was immediately sent to surgery. She was shaking with fear for him and walked by the chapel, hearing our worship music. She came in and was quickly encouraged as she realized God had provided a support team for her while she waited for her husband in surgery.

Worship to bring the presence of God in the chapel is key to lifting burdens. It is uplifting to our hearts, and the anointing of the Lord breaks every yoke. People come to the chapel to find help in desperate health situations and find a refreshing presence that makes their stresses not seem so burdensome after all. It is a place of peace where the sacrifice of praise has been made even in suffering, and the peace of God brings emotional freedom and victory. The Lord even anoints their minds with the oil of gladness.

Let the Lord's love touch your heart with healing. As in Psalm 91:1, He that dwells in the secret place of the Lord will dwell in the shadow of the almighty. Let the Almighty cover you and protect you. Let even the dark days of affliction bring no fear, because the wings of the Lord's presence cover you and shadow you from the fiery trials of life. Abide with Him in the stillness of this place and find the healing peace of God. Let it calm your fears, your anger, your heart, your blood pressure, and the stresses that compound disease. Let all who are weary come and find rest. Our yolk is easy and our burden is light when we abide in Him.

Truly, goodness and mercy shall follow us when we enter His presence. And we will walk out with His refreshing presence, trusting that He leads us beside still waters and restores our soul. Our cells will align with His Spirit and our body will be revived. There will be no depression because the Lord lifts our spirits. He is our Good Shepherd that leads us beside the still waters where we experience His peace and hear His still voice as we draw near to Him.

Let His love captivate your spirit and cleanse your spirit of all emotions that rob your peace and destiny. Let His light shine on your face that you would behold Him. May the Lord bless you and keep you and give you peace. May He warm our spirits, comfort our souls, and heal our diseases that we would be at *ease*, not *dis*ease. Let us come into Your presence together that we would have unity among us.

We pray that our differences would subside as we worship together. Let the Spirit and Bride invite all to come to His banqueting table. Your loving presence draws us with Your loving kindness. Show us great and mighty things to come in the earth and in our lives. Let destinies be fulfilled.

Delight in Him as He delights in you. Receive His love. Feel His pleasure over you. Feel His touch again. Feel His healing touch. Let Him restore feelings again. Feel His passion and joy over you and find peace and joy that surpasses disease, an abnormal condition that impairs bodily function with specific symptoms and signs. This can be internal or external environmental disease; any condition that causes pain, dysfunction, or social problems.

The altar is a place of peace and rest that you may come to God in the midst of your trial and find rest for your soul. It is a place where Father God says, "It will be all right. It is in My hands." Father God is waiting for you to come to Him in your time of need. He says, "I am with you, and you can rest in My arms in this place."

Even in the midst of bad news—know that all is well with your soul. He is with you no matter what you are going through, He is with you, and it will be OK.

Renewal of the Mind, Restoring the Heart

Spiritual transformation of nations comes with the renewal of people's minds. New peace and life come as new spiritual insights are discovered to bring new life and health. Families come to the chapel after getting devastating prognoses from their doctors. They come out of desperation because they need help from God to cope with what they have heard. Then, in the meditative healing atmosphere, the burden of it seems to lift and they get new hope in God. It is a mind-transforming experience as they are lifted from despair to hope and trust that God will be with them in it. God is our refuge and help in times of need. He is the Holy Comforter and Healer of body, soul, and spirit. Their minds are filled with new hope in the greatest physician, Jehovah Rapha. They realize new ways to pray. They can submit to the report of the doctor, and they can appeal to God for help and listen for the report of the Lord.

A teenage boy received a diagnosis of a rapidly growing tumor with a grim prognoses, and was already reported to be at end stage. They were devastated as they processed the medical report, but as soon as they received healing prayer, their hope was renewed. Blood tests started to improve and their outlook did, too. Soon, the young boy started getting his chemo treatments and was still going to athletic events. He started blogging about the good medical reports he was getting. Teenagers' faiths were being renewed as they read his blogs.

At the same time, a middle-aged woman got news of an abdominal tumor, also seriously progressed at diagnosis. She immediately called the prayer team with the play-by-play of her devastating news. But as the prayer team collected around her, she could smile and praise God even in the midst of the chemo process. She pulled out all the verses she had gotten as promises for her life and help onto them as weapons of warfare against the cancer cells.

Hope was restored and expectations renewed as to what God would do in her healing process.

Let the Lord God refresh and restore your heart and life that you could live an abundant life of good health and well-being. *"I pray that you may prosper in all things and be in health, just as your soul prospers*" (3 John 2). I close with the priestly Aaronic blessing:

> *The Lord bless you and keep you; the Lord make His face shine upon you, and be gracious to you. The Lord lift up His countenance upon you, and give you peace* (Numbers 6:24-26).

Appendix A

Healing Prayer Team Training

Theological Reasoning

There is power in the healing touch of the Lord through His people that can be accessed as we lay hands on the sick and pray (James 5:28). Believers have the authority of the Lord to speak healing words that can heal beyond what medicine can do. Psalms 103 clearly states the Lord forgives all our iniquities and heals all our diseases and we pray in full faith in the word of God that he will do it for those who come to him. The rest is up to the Lord in how he manifests His healing work in their lives. The Scriptures clearly state that God is the source of healing, and we pray believing prayers that He will bring a healing touch to each one.

Praying in a Medical Chapel

Healing team leaders need to negotiate a space with the medical staff leadership or pastoral care program. It generally works well for the prayer leader to work under the leadership of a doctor or chaplain who can give oversight to the ministry in the medical facility. Prayer ministers can volunteer under the auspices of the pastoral care chaplaincy department but be accountable to their pastoral prayer team leader. Prayer teams often are composed of people who carry their own healing testimonies and healing compassion and want to help others. They must behave in a manner that honors the house they are in and cooperates with medical center policies. Prayer in the chapel can be open Christian prayer because people have come to the chapel for a Christian healing ministry. Even Muslims and people of other faiths or those without faith seem to want healing prayer in the name of Jesus, as they believe that Jesus was a good Man that healed.

Team Selection

Prayer team members are selected as mature believers from various churches to represent the regional churches surrounding the medical facility. They are recommended by their pastors and are required to get four kinds of training:

1. Hospital volunteer training program
2. Hospital pastoral care training
3. Team healing prayer training utilizing healing rooms teaching by Cal Pierce, Mahesh Chavda's *Healing Prayer* text, Randy Clark's *Healing School Training,* and other healing teachings for team sharpening.
4. Ministry by supervision and direction of the team leader as they are assigned to assist an experienced ministry team member.

People are released for ministry by the team leader as they demonstrate their giftedness to be able to minister to the sick while honoring the medical setting. However, they still minister as directed and assigned by the pastoral leader who oversees the healing service. Those not ready for ministry may sit quietly in the room and pray but are not released to be prayer ministers. People need to have a good understanding of the healing scriptures, and an ability to show mercy and grace to the sick and suffering. Criteria for dismissal would be anyone who is unable to cooperate with the healing prayer team or medical facility policies and procedures.

Hosting the Glory of the Lord

As we pray in the designated chapel, we are establishing in a medical setting *"…a holy priesthood, offering spiritual sacrifices…"* and ministering to the people with the authority of the Kingdom of God (1 Pet. 2:5 NIV). We are a royal priesthood denoting our standing in Christ. Since we, the saints of God, have received sanctification of the spirit we are "holy," or set apart to offer our spiritual prayers before the Lord.

> *I beseech you therefore, brethren, by the mercies of God, that you present your bodies a living sacrifice, holy, acceptable to God, which is your reasonable service* (Romans 12:1).

Our spiritual sacrifices are doing good and ministering healing gifts to ones in need. This reasonable service is an analogy of divine service of the priests of Israel.

The priests carried a high authority, and we should see ourselves as carrying that authority in the spirit. Our prayers are powerful and effective as royal representatives of the Kingdom. The words we speak are heard in the heavenlies, and the Lord carries out His will in response to the powerful and effectual prayers we pray.

As we continue the prayers at the altar of God, we are hosting His presence and glory in that place. And as we stay connected to Him, we are servants of God doing inner court and outer court ministry to the Lord. We carry high authority as we host His presence as His priestly servants in our ministry.

Building a Healing Prayer Altar

Weekly meditative healing worship builds an altar of God's presence where the team can do inner and outer court ministry, worshiping God and stirring the atmosphere for healing while preparing the team's hearts to receive all who come to the altar for healing. Activities include live instrumental worship or CDs, worship dancers dressed in white, the healing ministry team, and intercessors. A hospitality person is posted at the door to receive people, a pastoral minister shares the healing word of God and orchestrates the ministry as people come, and prayer ministers are ready to respond to their needs. Small teams cluster around people to pray. One person leads the prayer team for each person to whom we minister, and the ministry team responds to needs as they come, keeping an atmosphere of worship going while they minister. Periodically, Scripture is read by the pastoral leader or other team members along a central theme for the day, such as peace, joy, comfort, or God's healing touch. As requests are made, small teams of two to four go to the rooms to pray over patients in their rooms. Remember, there are people of all faiths or no faith coming. They are generally in dire need of God's help for a loved one and need a healing, reviving touch of God to their body, mind, and spirit.

Team Purpose—Imparting the Father's Heart

1. Ask about the prayer need and how they want you to pray about it.

   Determine if they have a diagnosis to pray about or if they need wisdom to know what the diagnosis is. People can have the same medical situation but different ways they want you to pray. For example, one family with a loved one very ill may want prayer for healing, but another family in the same situation might feel the battle has been long enough and they may be ready to release their loved one. They may want prayers for wisdom in treatment.

2. Pray for root issues in their situation.

    They may ask for prayer for hypertension, but when you pray you may realize they have stress in their life that needs prayer. The stress may be the root cause of the hypertension, so the prayers will be most effective if they focus on removing the stress and bringing a spirit of peace that overcomes the hypertension. Ask what was happening in their lives when they first noticed the symptoms and get clues on the root issues in their lives that may need healing.

3. Ask about faith response.

    Ask if their faith is helping them through the health issue. Get a sense of their perspective on what God is doing in the sickness. Some think He is punishing them, or some think He is strengthening them.

4. Ask about the family.

    Do others have the same health issues?

5. Pray for God's wisdom and revelation about their situation.

    God may give a significant word that can help their healing. He could give a verse as a prescription for healing. When we were praying for a man with cancer God gave the verse, *"...I will never leave you nor forsake you"* (Josh. 1:5 NIV). When we shared this word with the patient who was at end-stage cancer he found great comfort in the promise that God would never leave him nor forsake him. We prayed that word into his spirit, and the word had a great healing effect. A week later, medical tests revealed a miraculous healing.

6. Lay hands on and anoint them with healing balm, first asking permission to do so.

    Most people welcome it, but some are uncomfortable with the idea (especially Catholics, since it may represent last rites to them) and have differing beliefs about what it means. Only move forward with anointing with oil if they are comfortable with it.

7. Pray encouraging, edifying prayers.

Even if you sense something negative, always pray the positive, encouraging thing. For example, if you sense fear over them pray for a spirit of peace to rest upon them. If you sense lack of faith pray for faith to arise and God to strengthen them.

8. Ask for feedback as to how they feel in response to the prayer.

Most people notice positive feelings and improvements in their body or spirit. This will direct you to further things to pray for their complete healing. Keep praying for symptoms to improve and both of you to feel the prayers have covered them. Continuing prayer can bring progressive healing. Ask them to check themselves for symptoms disappearing. Healing can begin on a cellular level and healing signs could be noticeable during prayer. Or ask them to get up and do what they couldn't have done with the sickness if they sense a strengthening of the spirit in their body. For example, ask them to get up and walk if they sense a strengthening in their legs and compulsion to do it. Faith in action helps the healing to manifest itself in fullness. Jesus often asked people to do an action to show faith and for them to realize signs of their own healing.

9. Command sickness to go.

When petitioning prayer stops working, pray commanding prayers to loose demonic activity if you sense a spirit of affliction has contributed to chronic sickness. When Jesus gave the great commission he spoke *"these signs will follow those who believe, in my name they will cast out demons...they will lay hands on the sick and they will recover"* (Mark 16:17-18). If strange manifestations occur, ask the Holy Spirit to take care of them. Tell demonic spirits to go quietly without creating a scene. Keep eyes open to pray and watch what is happening, remembering the Spirit of God in you has authority over it and you can quietly command it to go, expecting a quiet response. We do have authority over them. Use the authority you have. If they don't submit, tell them to submit in the name of Jesus. Encourage the believer to take control over it themselves as well. People should be actively involved in taking authority over anything out of spiritual alignment in their body or life.

10. Confess sin.

    Some people will need to confess a sin to loose the healing. James 5:16 calls us to confess our sins and the prayers will make the sick person well. Confessions bring the truth to the light and break the power of sin hidden in darkness. Freedom and healing come as the burden of guilt is relieved. Just as Jesus has the authority to forgive, we can dispel their guilt, saying, "Your sins are forgiven." He forgives *all* our iniquities and heals *all* our diseases. As you hear confessions, have an attitude of grace and compassion for them as you call them to sin no more, like Jesus did.

11. Remind them to keep praying and believing God's healing Word over their lives.

    Give verses for them to hold onto as direct promises from God's Word. Verses keep their faith strong and align their body with God's healing Word.

12. Ask them to come back and let you know the results. Many people do return with reports of healing, even though they have been discharged. They are thankful enough that they want to share their good news.

    Show genuine interest in the healing benefits of the prayer in their lives. Feedback of healings builds their faith and causes the testimony to be repeated in other people's lives. For example, if we have someone in the room who has been healed of cancer, we ask them to pray for another person struggling with cancer. Their healed testimony causes faith to arise for the next person's healing.

Boundaries

Nursing boundaries, first addressed by Florence Nightingale, are referred to in the "Nightingale Pledge." Passages such as, "I will abstain from whatever is deleterious and mischievous... maintain and elevate the standard of my profession...will hold in confidence matters committed to my keeping...in the practice of my calling...and devote myself to the welfare of those committed to my care," all refer to standards or boundaries relating to duties and responsibilities as nurses.[1] The American Nurse Association states, "When acting within one's role as a professional, the nurse recognizes and maintains boundaries that establish appropriate limits to relationships."[2]

Prayer ministers need to maintain similar boundaries in ministering to people. Being sensitive to personal boundaries of confidentiality should be maintained even in sharing prayer requests. Only offer prayer ministry they feel comfortable in receiving, and ask whether they feel comfortable with anointing or laying on of hands. Don't force personal revelations you might feel like sharing. Let them know what you would like to do and watch to see if they are comfortable as you carry it out. Pull back if they show signs of feeling uncomfortable.

A man came for prayer who knew he had a veiled heart and wanted to break through it. He wanted the veil lifted in prayer so he could have an open heart. He received prayer ministry with peace and joy for a while until he felt overwhelmed by it and drew back. The team needed to be sensitive to the boundary he put out, but they were eager to tell him more of their revelation to help him. It was overload to him, and he ran out. We need to be sensitive and not overwhelm people, even with good prayers that may be comfortable in our prayer circles but not to the new person unfamiliar with prayer ministry. Crossing therapeutic boundaries can happen when we are focused more on our prayer need than the personal reactions of the people to whom we are ministering.

Maintaining the Healing Benefits

Healing will be retained as people continue to have a right relationship with God and with others. They should walk in love and dispel deeds of darkness and put off unrighteous attitudes like bitterness or deceptiveness. Continuing to meditate on scriptural truths and live by them is to hear the words of the Lord and have them impact their faith walk as wholly healed people.

How to Bring Healing to Others

The power of the spoken word and the laying on of hands are a healing combination that imparts the Word and the healing touch. Jesus commands, *"Heal the sick, cleanse the lepers..."* (Matt. 10:8). The tongue of the wise promotes health. There is a voice of healing as believers speak that brings the power of God to save people out of their diseases and distresses. He sent His Word and healed them. Let the healing water of the Word wash over you and bring healing on a cellular level. Let your cells be restored in the name of Jesus. Let your spirit be lifted and let your body arise in wholeness and health in the name of Jesus.

God put His Spirit on His Servant, Jesus. Power went out from Him and he healed everyone with healing needs. With the power and anointing of the Lord, help people get in the healing pool when the waters are stirred up. Jesus touched eyes and said, *"According to your faith let it be to you,"* and their eyes were opened

(Matt. 9:29). The healing touch activates as the result of faith. As the anointed one touches the person with faith, the connection sends a healing power surge from Heaven.

How People Receive and Retain Healing

People ask, "How can I receive healing from God?" Those with physical health crises or emotional despair are driven to prayer when they might not have done it previously. In our most despairing situations, we cry out to God for healing. Our distress causes us to seek a supernatural source to alleviate our symptoms, especially when medicine has a poor prognosis for us. Jesus was moved by compassion to pray for people's healing. His compassion is a direct reflection of the heart of God for them, and it stirs the power of God to flow to release their healing. The outpouring of the Father's compassion for them brings power to heal and a loving atmosphere to receive the healing. People respond to the compassion and open their hearts to receive healing.

There is a yielding or surrendering in a person's heart and spirit that opens them to receive the outpouring of healing. Think of the woman with the issue of blood that knew she had to reach out to touch the hem of Jesus' robe to receive the healing virtue from Him. Her heart was open and ready to receive, so her reaching out just made a point of contact for her to receive. He noticed she touched Him, and He turned and commented, *"Who touched Me?"* He felt the flow of power go out from His Spirit, and He knew her faith in touching His robe would become the foundation for her to be able to receive the healing (see Luke 8:45). That is how faith works for healing. It opens our hearts to receive the healing virtue of God.

For emotional injuries, we let the light of Christ dispel the darkness in our soul: *"If the Son makes you free, you shall be free indeed"* (John 8:36).

The true source of emotional pain is our reaction to what is done unto us. Releasing grudges and blessing those who have hurt us causes a healing cycle in our lives. Forgiving releases God to work in them and God's forgiveness to us. Then blessing others brings blessing back to us.

The Healing Anointing

The power of God flows through the impartation of the laying on of hands and the presence of His Spirit in the atmosphere of worship and word. His love endures forever and He anoints my head with oil. The anointing flows from the throne of God above the heavens. It flows down over the mountains like the refreshing dew of Hermon descending the mountain of Zion, for there the Lord commands the blessing of life forevermore, as described in Psalms 133, into the people who need it.

We also carry a perfumed anointing oil as described in Psalms 23. *"You anoint my head with oil"* (Ps. 23:5). This is a refreshing, reviving anointing of mercy and grace from the loving kindness of the Good Shepherd who brings us to His perfect rest and restoration. This psalm portrays a person at peace in the Lord's dwelling place. His presence is so settling to the spirit even in the face of the threat of dying. You sense the Good Shepherd is close to guide and guard you with His staff, and you feel comforted. The Shepherd provides a daily restoration for the anxious, weary person. We carry His peace in our heart and carry His presence.

As He establishes His peaceable Kingdom, the Lord will set His hand to recover his people (see Isa. 11:11). He will set up a banner for the nations and assemble the outcasts of Israel and gather together the dispersed of Judah from the four corners of the earth. We carry His authority as we speak words for health and healing to our bodies. We can read, meditate, and speak them over ourselves as medicine to our spirit and soul. Let the words cause faith to increase. Faith and healing come by hearing the Word of God and receiving it as healing medicine into our beings. It is supernaturally natural, as it speeds up the healing on a cellular level in our bodies.

Guidelines for Giving *Rhema* Words

> *Now we have received, not the spirit of the world, but the Spirit who is from God, that we might know the things that have been freely given to us by God. These things we also speak, not in words which man's wisdom teaches but which the Holy Spirit teaches...* (1 Corinthians 2:12-13).

Words of knowledge are supernatural revelation of information received through the Holy Spirit apart from natural knowledge but by spiritual understanding. God gives this word about what He wants to heal. Ministering a word of knowledge is when a prayer minister senses a word of wisdom about a need a person has for healing. It reveals what God wants to heal and is often related to the underlying cause of the sickness, or it may be a word about what God may be doing in the healing process or family member. Generally it will build faith in the person needing healing, and it will move them to tears because it targets the core of their heart need that they may not have felt free to share, but God knew it was there and pinpointed it. People are moved that God is truly speaking to their heartfelt need and offering His solace in the process. It draws the hearts of the prayer team to the individual's need, and a sweet communion happens among the team and the sick. Often people want to hug and thank the prayer ministers because they feel so deeply encouraged and healed of concerns and sicknesses.

People need to use discretion in how to share a word of knowledge in a public place because many people haven't been exposed to such personal prayer and need it delivered in a tender, user-friendly way. We say, "As I was praying for you I had this sense that the Lord would want you to know..." and then the word of knowledge is shared. Or we may say, "I saw this picture as I prayed; does it make sense to you? I'll pray it for you." Interact in a way that they feel strengthened and edified by the word and the prayer that ensues.

1. *Words of knowledge should be consistent with the Bible.* You can speak God's promises over them to build faith in God's divine healing words, such as *"The prayer offered in faith will make the sick person well,"* and *"God forgives all our iniquities and heals all our diseases"* (see James 5:15 NIV; Ps. 103:3). These are truths from the Word that we can speak back to God to remind Him of His promises over our lives. But the *rhema* words of knowledge are personal diagnoses or prescriptions for what to do or what will come. A *rhema* word is God's confirmation of scriptural truths that God is applying for their personal life and situation.

2. Rhema words should be edifying and life-giving. We should speak things that lift their spirits and soothe their souls. The devil's strategy would be to kill, steal, and destroy. But the Lord's Word is to be life-giving to the spirit and soul.

3. *Rhema words should not ask people to stop cooperating with medical care.* They can give information to help the healing process or understand root causes, but they should not be antagonistic to the physician's plan. They may ask for the physician to redo some tests if you feel there is a healing resulting from prayer. We did pray for a man who was diagnosed with prostate cancer and we had a sense that he should have more tests because God was removing the cancer. So he asked for retesting after the prayer and found that the cancer was gone.

Patients Who Don't Recover

We have had families come to the chapel believing in full faith that their family members can be healed by God. We support them and their faith in prayer, even when they don't have hope from the doctor's prognosis. We pray to the end with them and support them. Many are healed, but some are not healed. The amazing response these families have builds our faith. They still thank us for the supportive prayers that gave them emotional and spiritual strength through the tough times of losing their loved ones. Sometimes, they even invite us to the funerals because of the deep hope and help we were in supporting them in their time of need. Jesus said, *"You were there for Me when I was hungry, and you clothed Me when I needed clothes. You did it when you ministered to the least of these, My people"* (see Matt. 25:33-40).

The prayers still give them comfort and strength so much that they have deep gratitude and never seem to forget the deep connection made with us and God during their time of need.

Hope Does Not Disappoint

Now hope does not disappoint, because the love of God has been poured out in our hearts by the Holy Spirit who was given to us (Romans 5:5).

We can have a peace with God that says, "It is well with my soul," knowing that there is a grace that we can hold onto as we rejoice in hope of the glory of God in our lives. God's love for us always seeks our highest good. There is a confidence we can hold onto that our concerns are in God's loving hands, and we release our burdens to Him knowing He will take care of them.

My daughter experienced a six-month pregnancy that ended in a stillbirth. As we held that baby in our arms, we grieved over a baby gone so young. It was hard to comprehend a life ended before it began. We had a service with other mothers who lost their babies prematurely and grieved over the loss of life. Still wondering what God was doing, but trusting our grandbaby was in His loving arms, I had a vision of our baby playing ring-around-the-rosie with the other babies, frolicking and having fun with the other babies who had lost their lives. Another life was lost through a family trauma, and I had a sense our baby had been a comfort and joy to the other baby and its mother. At the Lord's return, we will see the fullness of His glory and exult in seeing Him and realizing our part in His glory.

God's love has a bigger design than we can comprehend. It has goodness we don't understand as we look at our sufferings, but it has a hope of glory that in hindsight shows how God truly did work good in it for our lives and His glory.

Endnotes

1. Marilyn R. Peterson, *At Personal Risk: Boundary Violations in Professional-Client Relationships* (New York: W.W. Norton and Company, 1992), 182.

2. American Nurses Association, "Code of Ethics," NursingWorld, 2.4 Professional Boundaries, http://nursingworld.org/ethics/code/protected_nwcoe813.htm#1.2 (accessed March 29, 2010).

Appendix B

The Power of the Healing Word

The Word of God is a personal word to each of us to guide our faith and righteous behavior. His Word is His promises and truths that we can hold onto in faith and believe in what He says we can do and what He will do. Notice, many truths are interactive between our faith and God. We can pray His words back to Him as promises we hold onto in faith. He says hope in His Word will not disappoint. Select verses that speak to your heart for your healing need and pray them over your body, soul, spirit, life, and health. God's Word is alive forevermore.

Who Heals Us?

...I am the Lord who heals you (Exodus 15:26).

I will take sickness away from the midst of you. ...I will fulfill the number of your days (Exodus 23:25-26).

And the Lord will take away from you all sickness, and will afflict you with none of the terrible diseases of Egypt which you have known... (Deuteronomy 7:15).

...The Lord your God turned the curse into a blessing for you, because the Lord your God loves you (Deuteronomy 23:5).

The Lord will give strength to His people; the Lord will bless His people with peace (Psalms 29:11).

The Lord will preserve him and keep him alive, and he will be blessed on the earth (Psalms 41:2).

...for I shall yet praise Him, the help of my countenance and my God (Psalms 43:5).

With long life I will satisfy him, and show him My salvation (Psalms 91:16).

Our Foundation for Healing

He himself bore our sins in His body on the tree, so that we might die to sins and live for righteousness; by His wounds you have been healed (1 Peter 2:24 NIV).

Our Authority to Pray

Behold, I give you the authority to trample on serpents and scorpions, and over all the power of the enemy, and nothing shall by any means hurt you (Luke 10:19).

And these signs will follow those who believe: In My name they will cast out demons...they will lay hands on the sick, and they will recover (Mark 16:17-18).

Our Faith for Healing

Now faith is the substance of things hoped for, the evidence of things not seen (Hebrews 11:1).

And the prayer of faith will save the sick, and the Lord will raise him up. And if he has committed sins, he will be forgiven (James 5:15).

Therefore I say to you, whatever things you ask when you pray, believe that you receive them, and you will have them (Mark 11:24).

And whatever you ask in My name, that I will do, that the Father may be glorified in the Son. If you ask anything in My name, I will do it (John 14:13-14).

Heal me, O Lord, and I shall be healed; save me, and I shall be saved (Jeremiah 17:14).

"Return, you backsliding children, and I will heal your backslidings." "Indeed we do come to You, for You are the Lord our God" (Jeremiah 3:22).

Behold, I will bring it health and healing; I will heal them and reveal to them the abundance of peace and truth (Jeremiah 33:6).

Come, and let us return to the Lord; for He has torn, but He will heal us; He has stricken, but He will bind us up (Hosea 6:1).

I will heal their backsliding, I will love them freely, for My anger has turned away from him (Hosea 14:4).

But to you who fear My name the Sun of Righteousness shall arise with healing in His wings; and you shall go out and grow fat like stall-fed calves (Malachi 4:2).

And Jesus went about all Galilee, teaching in their synagogues, preaching the Gospel of the Kingdom, and healing all kinds of sicknesses and all kinds of diseases among the people (Matthew 4:23).

Then Jesus said to the centurion, "Go your way; and as you have believed, so let it be done for you." And his servant was healed that same hour (Matthew 8:13).

When evening had come, they brought to Him many who were demon-possessed. And He cast out the spirits with a word, and healed all who were sick (Matthew 8:16).

And when He had called His twelve disciples to Him, He gave them power over unclean spirits, to cast them out, and to heal all kinds of sickness and all kinds of disease (Matthew 10:1).

Heal the sick, cleanse the lepers, raise the dead, cast out demons. Freely you have received, freely give (Matthew 10:8).

Then one was brought to Him who was demon-possessed, blind and mute; and He healed him, so that the blind and mute man both spoke and saw (Matthew 12:22).

And when Jesus went out he saw a great multitude; and He was moved with compassion for them, and healed their sick (Matthew 14:14).

And the whole multitude sought to touch Him, for power went out from Him and healed them all (Luke 6:19).

So they departed and went through the towns, preaching the Gospel and healing everywhere (Luke 9:6).

Whatever city you enter, and they receive you, eat such things as are set before you. And heal the sick there, and say to them, "The kingdom of God has come near to you" (Luke 10:8-9).

And one of them, when he saw that he was healed, returned, and with a loud voice glorified God (Luke 17:15).

Now when the woman saw that she was not hidden, she came trembling; and falling down before Him, she declared to Him in the presence of all the people the reason she had touched Him and how she was healed immediately (Luke 8:47).

Daughter, be of good cheer; your faith has made you well... (Luke 8:48).

...And the power of the Lord was present to heal them (Luke 5:17).

The Lord Heals You

"For I will restore health to you and heal you of your wounds," says the Lord... (Jeremiah 30:17).

No weapon formed against you shall prosper, and every tongue which rises against you in judgment you shall condemn. This is the heritage of the servants of the Lord... (Isaiah 54:17).

Beloved, I pray that you may prosper in all things and be in health, just as your soul prospers (3 John 1:2).

O Lord my God, I cried out to You, and You healed me (Psalms 30:2).

Have mercy on me, O Lord, for I am weak; O Lord, heal me, for my bones are troubled (Psalms 6:2).

He sent his word and healed them, and delivered them from their destructions (Psalms 107:20).

He heals the brokenhearted and binds up their wounds (Psalms 147:3).

…Fear the Lord and depart from evil. It will be health to your flesh, and strength to your bones (Proverbs 3:7-8).

Faith in God's Word Brings Healing

My son, give attention to my words; incline your ear to my sayings. …For they are life to those who find them, and health to all their flesh (Proverbs 4:20,22).

Now faith is the substance of things hoped for, the evidence of things not seen (Hebrews 11:1).

…I will take sickness away for the midst of you (Exodus 23:25).

Declare, "I am healed in Christ Jesus. By His stripes I am healed. I shall live to declare the works of the Lord. For greater is Jesus that he that is in the world."

Special Prayer for Healing

Lord, we bow before Your presence, thanking You for Your great love for us and Your finished work on the Cross. Reveal Your full Gospel that is the foundation and source of healing in our lives. Reveal to us any sin in our hearts that might hinder our receiving Your healing. And open our hearts to bow before You and repent. Heal our land, heal our lives, heal our bodies, heal our relationships, for You are our Lord and Savior. We claim Your promises of health and healing for our bodies, minds, and spirits.

My son, pay attention to what I say; listen closely to my words. Do not let them out of your sight; keep them within your heart; for they are life to those who find them and health to a man's whole body (Proverbs 4:20-22 NIV).

Abide in the Lord and His Healing Virtue

I am the vine, you are the branches. He who abides in Me, and I in him, bears much fruit; for without Me you can do nothing (John 15:5).

Come abide in the wellspring of His presence and draw sustenance to your body, soul, and spirit! Find the abundant life that Jesus came to bring; let it gush forth in your life and overflow to other's lives. Bring the delight of the Lord to your life and around the world!

Friends, the real message in these healing stories, and all the healing stories or Scripture, reminds us that whether He is among his disciples or the crowds, whether He is in Galilee or out among Gentiles, whether He is trying to get a respite or working hard, Jesus cares about healing and wholeness. You can say many things about Jesus—He was a teacher, a prophet, a rabbi, a healer. But, the real message in these healing stories is His great redemptive love for us! Healing blessings to you!

Abby Abildness,
founder and director of Healing Tree International

ABOUT ABBY ABILDNESS

You can email at:

Abby@HealingTreeInternational.com

Website: www.HealingTreeInternational.com